STORIES OF THE UNDERGROUND RAILROAD

By
ANNA L. CURTIS

Foreword
RUFUS M. JONES

♥

Illustrated by William Brooks

♥

NEW YORK
THE ISLAND WORKSHOP PRESS CO-OP., INC.
1941

COPYRIGHT 1941
THE ISLAND WORKSHOP PRESS
CO-OP., INC.

CHARLES A. PHELPS DESIGN-PRODUCTION
PRINTED IN UNITED STATES OF AMERICA

Printing Statement:

Due to the very old age and scarcity of this book, many of the pages may be hard to read due to the blurring of the original text, possible missing pages, missing text and other issues beyond our control.

Because this is such an important and rare work, we believe it is best to reproduce this book regardless of its original condition.

Thank you for your understanding.

FOREWORD

by Rufus M. Jones

♥

THESE STORIES of scenes and events in the work of *"The Underground Railroad"* will delight readers of all ages. They are excellent boys' and girls' stories, but the older members of the family will like them just as much as the young people. They are "stories," but they are not imaginary. They happened. These men and women, these boys and girls, are real persons and they did these brave deeds herein related.

The heroic element is very much in evidence. Every event involved risk and danger. Thomas Garrett was made poor by his courageous actions; all these characters faced fines and imprisonment, or worse, every time they aided a slave to escape. There was no fame or public glory in what they were doing. "Fame" would have instantly defeated all their endeavors. They did not let the left hand know what the right hand was doing. Their nearest neighbors were kept

FOREWORD

ignorant of their risky deeds of love. The newspapers had no headlines and no local items of their proceedings. Often the poor hunted "railroad passenger"—and God—were all who knew.

These stories will remind us of the fact that modern Quakers are not the only ones who have taken up the burden of the world's suffering. We of today are only carrying on a torch which our forebears handed down to us, lighted and burning. They were faithful in their day and generation, and they were bearers of light in the darkness of their times. Our tasks are very different; but they call for that same old-time spirit of faithfulness.

These "conductors" on the Underground Railroad had an interesting technique of truth-telling. They would not deviate from the truth to save their lives. One cannot find a *lie* in all the records. The words they spoke were words of truth, but they often gave a "false impression" to the man-hunters with whom they had to deal. They "deceived" them with their "truth." They put them off the track, and yet their words did not lie. Is it "all right" for a lone woman in a house to have a man's hat on the hat-rack by the door to warn off a dangerous caller, and may she shout upstairs to "John" when there isn't any "John" up there? Is it all right to put your hand over your patched elbow when you want to make the impres-

FOREWORD

sion of respectability? When does a "deceit" become a "lie"? That is a question each person settles with his own conscience, and these tender-minded truth-tellers had the approval of their inner tribunals.

Their course of violating the law of the land, as they often did, was more dubious. They were under the empire of a higher law, and they felt that they could not "do otherwise." In all ages of hard crisis there have been persons who have said, "We must obey God rather than men." There have been persons who have felt an irresistible inner urge, which seemed to come out of eternity, to go against wrong that had the sanction of law. The prophet does it; the saint does it; the martyr does it. And these persons did it. But it must never be easily done, or boastingly done. It is often a tragic course to take, and calls for profound spiritual depth of life, and readiness to take the consequences. These stories are about persons of that type.

RUFUS M. JONES

·WHERE THE STORIES CAME FROM

THE TEN STORIES in this collection and the biographical sketch of THOMAS GARRETT ("Our Moses") first appeared five or six years ago in the children's paper, *Scattered Seeds,* of Philadelphia, Pennsylvania, which has given gracious permission for their publication in book form. The sketch was written from material furnished by Garrett's granddaughter, Helen S. Garrett.

The background account, "THE RAILROAD AND ITS PASSENGERS," is derived from many sources, including Henrietta Buckmaster's recent fine book, "Let My People Go."

Most of the stories printed in *Scattered Seeds* were told to me by members of families who participated in the events related. As is only to be expected, the majority are tales of hairbreadth escapes, for dramatic events pass easily down in family tradition, while less exciting facts, such as weeks of feeding the hungry

WHERE THE STORIES CAME FROM

and helping those in flight, may pass into oblivion.

The story "WAJELMA" is rewritten from Lydia Maria Child's "Life of Isaac T. Hopper," from which also was taken material for the sketch of his life given here.

"THE ROAD TO CANADA" comes from the "Autobiography" of Allen Jay, of Indiana. Most of the conversation in the story is taken from his own account of the events.

The sketch of LEVI COFFIN is based on his own "Reminiscences." From this source also comes "A STATION ON THE UNDERGROUND RAILROAD."

"THE STORY OF FRANK QUAINTANCE" was told to me by the nephew of Henry W. Wilbur who figured in the events as a child.

"A CASE OF WHOOPING COUGH" comes directly from the daughter of James and Amelia Jackson who were "conductors" at this "station" in Delaware. I myself remember the couple in later years, old, bowed, and feeble, yet retaining something of the fire which in their youth had made them staunch supporters of true freedom.

"BROWN SISTER" and "THE RUNAWAY SLAVE" are as related by Emily W. Lawton, who, though living in New York at the time of narrating, was born in Ohio, in a house which had been a busy Underground Railroad station.

WHERE THE STORIES CAME FROM

All these stories were approved in their final form by those who gave data for them.

"THE FACE AT THE WINDOW" was seen by my own grandmother in northern Ohio. This story and "THE HEARTHSTONE" and "DAVID GOES TO MARKET" are typical narratives of the Underground Railroad.

The account of HARRIET TUBMAN is taken largely from Elizabeth Ross Haynes' biography of this remarkable woman, in her book "Unsung Heroes."

Except for the biography of HARRIET TUBMAN and "A STATION ON THE UNDERGROUND RAILROAD," the stories are all of Quaker workers and their work. But no book about the Railroad can be just or true which does not bear testimony to the gallant part played by the Negroes themselves in securing freedom for others of their race.

There is still a great emancipation problem before us all. This time, however, our efforts may be made in the full light of day, to bring it about that color shall not count in the rights of citizenship or in our feeling of brotherhood toward each other. May Negroes and Whites continue to work side by side in the eternal struggle to maintain freedom for all. I shall be glad if in these pictures of the past there may be some inspiration for the future.

ANNA L. CURTIS.

CONTENTS

The Railroad and Its Passengers 1
Lawyer to the Negro: Isaac T. Hopper . . . 12
Wajelma 20
The Road to Canada 28
"President" of the Railroad: Levi Coffin . . 34
A Station on the Underground Railroad . . 40
The Story of Frank Quaintance 48
The Hearthstone 56
David Goes to Market 64
A Case of Whooping-Cough 72
"Conductor" on the Underground Railroad:
   Thomas Garrett 80
Brown Sister 88
The Runaway Slave 94
The Face at the Window 102
"Engineer" Who Never Lost a Passenger:
   Harriet Tubman 108

ALLEN AND HIS PASSENGER (THE ROAD TO CANADA, PAGE 28)

THE RAILROAD AND ITS PASSENGERS

❧

THE UNDERGROUND RAILROAD was the name by which the secret organization was known that helped escaping slaves to freedom in pre-Civil War days in the United States.

The "Railroad" had actually been operating for years before it received its name. In 1831 a slave named Tice Davids escaped from Kentucky. He came to the Ohio River, plunged in, and managed to swim across. His master was close on his heels, and finding a skiff, rowed after the bobbing head in the water. He was swiftly overtaking Tice when the slave touched bottom and waded ashore near the little town of Ripley. It seemed to the master only a matter of moments now until he would overtake him. But the slave disappeared, and though he was dripping wet, there was no trace of him anywhere. His master searched the locality in vain, and said ruefully, "He must have gotten away by an underground road."

In those days the steam railroad was new, and to many people mysterious. The supposition that perhaps a "railroad" figured in some way in the escape system was welcomed by the Quakers, whose activities must necessarily be veiled and secret. So the friends of escaping slaves completed the phrase, making it "The Underground Railroad," under which name the system operated until slaves were totally freed by the Civil War.

All the States north of Maryland soon after the Revolutionary War passed laws providing for setting their slaves free gradually. However, the Quakers and numerous other persons had freed their slaves even before the Constitution of the United States was adopted in 1789.

The Quakers, or Friends, had come to believe that it was wrong to hold people in slavery, whatever their color. Even as early as 1786, some Quakers were helping runaway slaves to reach places where they could live as free men. This was the small beginning of the Railroad. One incident that gave impetus to local organization occurred about twenty years later, when a runaway slave found refuge in Columbia, Pennsylvania. His mistress learned where he was, and came to demand that he be given back to her. She was so overbearing and rude in manner, and the

THE RAILROAD AND ITS PASSENGERS » 3

slave was so terrified at being taken back, that some inhabitants of the town determined to make sure that no other escaped slaves should be captured in Columbia.

Small groups in other towns and cities banded themselves together for the same purpose. The organization grew swiftly, but always secretly, for it was against the law to help a runaway slave. Even in States whose own Negroes had all become free, any escaped slave could be legally taken back by his master or by a professional slave-catcher, and any person who helped a slave to safety was liable to be punished if found out.

The first Fugitive Slave Law, of 1793, provided a fine of $500 upon anyone who helped a runaway slave. However, people in the Northern States paid less and less attention to this as time went on, and some of the States even passed their own laws ordering magistrates of the courts not to take any part in carrying out the Fugitive Slave Law.

So in 1850, Congress, which represented the slave owners as well as those opposed to slavery, passed the second Fugitive Slave Law, which provided that anyone who hid a slave or helped him to freedom might be fined $1000 or imprisoned for six months, and also might have to pay $1000 for each fugitive thus lost to the owner. A man in Baltimore was sentenced to forty-five years imprisonment for helping a slave family of nine to escape. Moreover, all officers of the law were required to help owners take their slaves back, and any citizen could be compelled under the law to help capture fugitives.

This law made it more dangerous than ever to help runaway slaves, but its unjustness also made more people eager to help them and see them all free.

In the early 1800's runaway slaves simply found homes and work in free States, and only once in a while would a determined owner pursue and find his slave and take him back. Many bought their freedom from their owners, or escaped again. Isaac T. Hopper and other workers in the Abolition Society helped many Negroes to do both.

However, as the years went on, and slaves escaped in increasing numbers, their owners became more earnest in pursuing them. And after the passage of the Fugitive Slave Law of 1850, there was no safety for them in the United States, so Canada was the goal of all. Thousands of runaways who had been settled in the North for years were forced to flee once more.

A hymn, based on God's message to Pharaoh, "Let my people go," was whispered from one slave to another on plantations. Forbidden by the masters as being too significant to suit them, it was sung aloud only when the Negroes found themselves in safety north of the Ohio River, or the Mason-Dixon Line.

> "Go down, Moses,
> 'Way down in Egypt Land,
> And tell old Pharaoh
> To let my people go."

As the number of escaping slaves increased, so grew the Underground Railroad. It was increasingly active up to the very beginning of the Civil War. Quakers were the leaders in the work. A discouraged slave-hunter once said, "It's as easy to find a needle in a haymow as a nigger among Quakers." But there were many other workers besides Quakers. Both Negroes and Whites co-operated in aiding escaping slaves. In Ohio a group of Presbyterian ministers were leaders in the work. Oberlin College was a source of helpfulness to the Negro. So was Lane Theological Seminary, at Cincinnati, Ohio. Numerous groups of free Negroes, as in Sandusky, handled fugitives without the aid of white men. There were helpers in the South itself, who would direct runaways to stations of the Railroad.

Also in the South there was growing emancipation sentiment, outspoken until opposing opinion became violent, and from the South came a great many of the country's leading anti-slavery workers. Many owners freed their slaves voluntarily, even at personal sacrifice. The number of free Negroes in slave-States increased steadily, from 32,000 in 1790 to 260,000 in 1860.

Both sections of the United States were equally responsible for the establishment of slavery. So said Lincoln in his great debate with Stephen Douglas. The fact that there were a larger number of slaves in the South than in the North can be attributed largely to climatic conditions. The Negro could thrive in the warm South, more nearly like his native climate, and could remain healthy, with less attention, housing and clothing, than he could in the colder North. This created an economic condition whereby the Southern slave-owner, with cheaply-kept labor, could produce and control goods and prices in such a manner that slavery was becoming a calamity for white men who were not slave owners and who were laborers or employers of free labor.

Led by those who hated slavery in its own name, fair-minded people, both North and South, were coming to the point of abolishing slavery by the mutual will of the people, but due to the hotheads on both sides of the line, this unfortunately was not to be, and the Civil War resulted.

New stations of the Underground Railroad were constantly springing up, as new sympathizers were

The Railroad and Its Passengers

found. A story is told of a white man guiding a Negro northward. They had been obliged to turn from their proper road, and knew of no helper now near. So the Negro hid in a swamp, while the white man went ahead to find a haven for him. Pretending that he was a slave-catcher, he asked a farmer if he had seen an escaping slave, whom he described. The farmer replied with a lecture on the right of Negroes to their freedom. That farmer was soon conducting a new station of the Railroad.

The Railroad became closely organized, yet it was rare that any "conductor" or "brakeman" knew the line of travel across his State. The less they knew the better. A family would know the last place, possibly ten to twenty miles away, from which fugitives came to them; and would know the place, or perhaps several places, to which they should next be sent. But that was all.

Only since the Civil War has it been possible to trace out the routes. Investigators have gone from station to station, and have worked out the network of routes northward to Canada, across all the Northern States, from Kansas to Maine. There were many sympathizers among the sailors along the coast. A runaway might be hidden in the hold of a vessel and brought to New Bedford or Marblehead, Massachusetts, or Portland, Maine, to go by land into Canada.

The most dangerous time for a runaway was before he reached a station of the Railroad. The mysterious "grapevine telegraphy" among the slaves had told them there were people in the North, both white and black, who would help them to freedom. A Negro might follow the North Star to a free State, but even then he might not know who were his friends and who were not. He would have to walk northward, living on roots and berries, until he came upon a station by chance or was directed to one by a free Negro. Many fugitives were retaken before they had found the Underground Railroad. But few indeed were captured after reaching a station.

The "conductors" developed the most amazing resourcefulness in hiding their passengers. Many constructed secret hiding-places. A cave might be cut into a hillside. A mill might have a hiding-place almost under the great water-wheel. Houses were equipped with false partitions, invisible doors, movable hearthstones.

A house near Marion, Ohio, had false partitions in both attic and cellar. The attic was a carefully constructed labyrinth. In the cellar there were two secret rooms, each large enough to hold a dozen refugees. From the cellar two underground tunnels led out, one to the barn, the other to the corn-crib, their ends so carefully concealed that searchers for slaves never came upon them. Several times Negroes escaped by these tunnels while their owners watched outside.

Nothing was ever written about the Railroad while it was in operation, and as little as possible was said about it. Women prepared baskets of food, and left them standing, "in case anybody should be hungry." Three or four families might have a common arrangement "for sending produce northward." One member of a family might hide a fugitive in the barn or the orchard, with no word to others of the family. If inquiry came, that person would keep out of the way, leaving others to answer questions. A direct lie could not be countenanced by these deeply religious people, so evasiveness was their shield. They could not tell what they did not know. They did not recognize slavery as an institution, so they could always truthfully say there were no "slaves" in their homes. If a questioner asked if Negroes were there, the "conductor" might reply, "Look and see," or "Thee will find no Negroes here." Thomas Garrett more than once simply refused to answer questions.

A child might be away from home unnoticed, while the absence of a grownup would have aroused suspicion. So a boy or girl of ten or eleven might be put on a horse with a fugitive behind, or put in charge of a wagon- or carriage-load, and sent off to the next station. Mordecai Benedict, of Marengo,

Ohio, began to drive fugitives northward when he was only six years old.

One little boy was called on for such service who did not even know the way to the next station. Danger was pressing for the runaway, and the grownups dared not go, for fear of betraying him. There was eighteen miles to travel, but the horse knew the way, and at the end of the route pushed open the gate into a certain lane. This was truly an instance where a horse's instinct assisted a man to freedom.

The four persons whose lives are sketched in this book are typical of hundreds of devoted servants of the cause of freedom. A few others should at least be named:

William Cratty, of Ohio, began his work in 1839, and during the next nine years helped 3,000 slaves northward.

Robert Purvis, in Philadelphia, helped an average of a fugitive a day for thirty years. From 1831 to 1861 he sent 9,000 slaves on their way to freedom.

William Still, also of Philadelphia, was the Negro secretary of an active line of the Underground Railroad. His passengers went from Philadelphia to Burlington, New Jersey, thence to Bordentown, and so to New Brunswick, Rahway, and Jersey City. From Jersey City they were taken to the railway station on 42nd Street, New York, where tickets were bought for them to continue their journey by rail to Syracuse.

Josiah Henson, like Harriet Tubman, was an escaped slave. Like her, too, he repeatedly dared to return South and lead groups of freedom-seekers. Numerous others went back to rescue their families, but these two went again and again. Henson acted as escort for over 200 runaway slaves. Harriet Beecher Stowe knew him well. It is said that it was he who inspired the character Uncle Tom in her great book, "Uncle Tom's Cabin." Henson escaped the fate of poor Uncle Tom, but in his sterling character, absolute honesty and strong Christianity, he was Uncle Tom himself.

All these people were constantly and deliberately disobeying a law of the land. Respected and otherwise law-abiding citizens, they insisted that *this* law defied the law of God, which declares that all men are brothers. In obedience to the law of God, they fed the hungry, sheltered the homeless, poured out money, time and strength, and constantly ran the risk of heavy fine and imprisonment.

The Underground Railway movement possessed a tremendous religious spirit. Its workers took literally Christ's sermon in Nazareth: "The Spirit of the Lord is upon me, because . . . he hath sent me to preach deliverance to the captives . . . to set at liberty them that are bruised."

LAWYER TO THE NEGRO: ISAAC T. HOPPER

❦

"Where did you come from, Uncle Mingo?" asked the little boy.

"From Africa," answered the old colored man. "They brought me over here when I was no bigger than you are now, and I've been a slave ever since."

"How did they do that?"

"A lot of us children were playing together on the shore when some white men jumped out of the bushes, and caught us, and dragged us off to a ship. We tried our best to get away. I held on to the thorn bushes until my hands were bleeding as if I had cut them with a knife. But the men pulled me away. None of us ever saw our fathers and mothers any more. I've been a slave all these long years."

Isaac T. Hopper was only nine years old when he talked with Uncle Mingo. But he was old enough to say to himself that if he ever had opportunity to help a Negro who was in trouble he would do so.

All his life he remembered this promise. He became known as the sure friend of the colored people. During the first half of the last century many colored men and women were living in Philadelphia who had escaped from slavery in the Southern States. They were in constant danger of being recognized by their former owners and carried back to slavery. There were frequent cases, too, where free Negroes were kidnaped and taken away to be sold. For forty years, Isaac Hopper was never sure of a night's rest. Again and again he was roused by some terrified Negro. Perhaps the cry would be, "The slave-catchers have found my husband and they have him in prison until they can prove he is a slave and take him away." Or perhaps he would be called to help a free man prove that he had always been free or had bought his right to freedom.

Isaac Hopper was only about sixteen years of age in 1787 when he helped the first of these unfortunates. A slave from Bermuda had been hired out by his master to work on a ship going to New York. But as soon as he reached port, the slave, named Joe, slipped away and walked to Philadelphia for safety. Unfortunately, on his first day in Philadelphia he ran into a friend of his master. The friend had no idea that Joe was trying to escape, but merely thought he had been left behind, and kindly offered to help him get back home. Young Isaac Hopper saw the two as they waited for the boat to Bermuda. He decided that Joe was really not as pleased at the prospect of returning home as he pretended to be.

Watching his chance, young Isaac whispered to the slave, "Do you really want to go back? You can count on me to be your friend and never betray you." The colored man looked at him long and earnestly. Isaac never forgot that look of distress. Then Joe told him the truth, and Isaac set himself about doing what he could to help him. He knew few people in Philadelphia, but he consulted a friendly neighbor and learned of a Quaker in the country who was a good friend of the colored people. Joe was given a letter to this Quaker, along with careful instructions how to reach him.

According to their plan, in order to avoid suspicion and pursuit, the Negro went aboard ship, but the next day was allowed to go ashore for some clothes he had purposely left behind. Once on shore, away from Philadelphia he went, walking all night long. The next morning he reached his destination safely and delivered Isaac's letter. He was kindly received, found a job, and lived as a free man for the rest of his life.

This was Isaac's first opportunity to help a Negro

LAWYER: ISAAC T. HOPPER   » 15

to freedom. Forty years later, he had saved over a thousand men and women. The colored people of Philadelphia believed in him absolutely. He knew all the laws connected with slavery so well that even lawyers found themselves no match for him. But when his knowledge of law was not enough, his mind worked like a flash, and again and again he helped fugitives to escape from under the very hands of their former masters.

On one occasion when an escaped slave was given haven in Isaac Hopper's home, his master came and set a guard before the house to prevent him escaping to the street. But Isaac Hopper had arranged for him to flee through the back of the house and over the backyard fence. The master was literally stretching out his hand toward his property when the slave bolted through the back door, turned the key which locked the door from the outside. Before the master could find another way to the rear of the house, the slave had climbed the fence and was out of sight.

Often Hopper's quick wits turned the tables on slaveholders in most unexpected fashion. Once a slave case was brought before a Judge Rush. The Judge seemed to favor the owner, and the unhappy Negro began to despair. Just then, Isaac Hopper said to the Judge: "Hast thou not recently published a legal opinion in which it is distinctly stated that thou wouldst never seek to sustain a human law if thou were convinced that it conflicted with any law in the Bible?"

"Yes," answered Judge Rush. "I did publish such a statement, and I am ready to abide by it; for in all cases I consider the divine law above the human law."

Calmly, Friend Hopper drew from his pocket a small Bible, and read aloud a couple of verses from the 23rd Chapter of Deuteronomy:

"Thou shalt not deliver unto his master the servant which is escaped from his master unto thee: He shall dwell with thee, even among you, in that place which he shall choose, in one of the gates, where it liketh him best; thou shalt not oppress him."

The slaveholder laughed. "Why should that old Hebrew law be brought into a modern court?" But when the Judge asked for the book, read the passage for himself, and then adjourned the decision of the case, the owner walked out of the courthouse muttering, "I believe in my soul the old fool will let him off on that ground." And surely enough, the slave was discharged.

So this friend of the Negro labored year after year. The first fugitive slave who was endangered by the Law of 1850 was saved by Isaac T. Hopper, then eighty years old, and living in New York. This slave

CAUTION!!
COLORED PEOPLE
OF BOSTON, ONE & ALL,

You are hereby respectfully CAUTIONED and advised, to avoid conversing with the

Watchmen and Police Officers of Boston,

For since the recent ORDER OF THE MAYOR & ALDERMEN, they are empowered to act as

KIDNAPPERS
AND
Slave Catchers,

Keep a Sharp Look Out for KIDNAPPERS, and have TOP EYE open.

APRIL 24, 1851.

THEODORE PARKER'S PLACARD

PLACARD WHICH WAS WRITTEN BY THEODORE PARKER AND POSTED BY THE VIGILANCE COMMITTEE AFTER THE RENDITION OF THOMAS SIMS TO SLAVERY IN APRIL, 1851.

had lived for several years in Worcester, Massachusetts, but had gone to New York to be married, on the very day that his former master arrived in Worcester to search for him. A friend of the colored man sent word to Isaac Hopper by telegraph. Though it arrived at midnight, Hopper sprang from his bed as he had done so often before, and hurried to warn the fugitive. The poor fellow feared it might be a trick to capture him, but his young wife looked earnestly at the face of the patriarch, and said, "I would trust that Quaker gentleman anywhere. Let us go with him."

They spent the rest of the night at the Hopper home, and a few days later went to Canada. Six months imprisonment and a fine of a thousand dollars was the penalty under the new law for anyone who should be convicted of aiding a runaway slave. But Friend Hopper said time and again:

"I have never tried to make any slave discontented with his situation, because I do not consider it either wise or kind to do so; but so long as my life is spared, I will always assist anyone who is trying to escape from slavery, be the laws what they may."

In 1852, Isaac T. Hopper died. He had been overseer of a school for colored children; volunteer teacher in a school for adult Negroes; lawyer and protector of slaves and colored people upon all occasions. But he did far more than this. The poor were continually calling upon him to plead with hardhearted landlords and creditors. In New York, for years, he was secretary of the newly formed Prison Association, to help men and women discharged from prison to find work and lead honest lives. The Isaac T. Hopper Home on Second Avenue in New York still helps women who have met with the law, and carries on the spirit of the man whom it commemorates. A friend once said of him: "The Bible requires us to love our neighbors as well as ourselves: Friend Isaac has loved them better."

WAJELMA

♥

IN THE DARK COOL BASEMENT of an old Philadelphia house a ten-year-old colored boy was bending over a pair of high riding-boots, rubbing them with all the strength of his thin, wiry arms. He was not only the apprentice of M. Genolles, a tailor, who had come from Paris many years before, but also his body-servant, as valets were often called in those days.

Wajelma owed his name to the tradition told him by his mother, that an ancestor of his own had been chief of a tribe in the heart of Africa, and was named Wajelma. His mother had been happy when the opportunity came for him to be apprenticed to M. Genolles, for it meant that he would have a good trade when he grew up.

M. Genolles was reasonably kind to him. The boy was seldom beaten, thanks to his quick hands and eyes. And he was not a slave. There were still some slaves in Pennsylvania in the year 1804, but Wajelma and his mother both were free.

Today Wajelma was worried. M. Genolles had told him that he was returning to France, and when the boy asked him about his apprenticeship, the reply was merely, "You'll find out in good time."

Wajelma was puzzling over this reply when suddenly a hand fell on his shoulder, and M. Genolles spoke sharply, "Quick, get those boots into the chest and lock it. The wind is up, and the boat will sail in an hour."

Wajelma's nimble hands made short work of the final packing and locking, but all the time he kept asking himself inwardly, "What about me? What am I to do?"

The carriage was at the door, the chest strapped on, and Wajelma stepped up to his master to wish him a good trip. "But you're coming to the ship with me," said M. Genolles. "I have something special for you there."

"I'll get my cap, sir," answered Wajelma, but his master snapped out, "There's no time. In with you!" He pulled the boy into the carriage and slammed the door. "To the packet, and hurry, man," he shouted to the driver, and they were off.

As they neared the docks, the spread sails of the

fast packet made a beautiful sight in Wajelma's eyes. Once on deck, he was no less interested, for this was his first visit to a large boat. His arms laden with cloaks and bundles, he followed M. Genolles down to the cabin, where several friends of his master, as well as other passengers, were congregated.

"Wait here in the corner for me," said M. Genolles, turning to greet his friends. Minutes went by ... a quarter-hour. Wajelma slipped timidly to M. Genolles' side. "May I say goodbye, sir, and wish you a pleasant journey?"

At that moment, they felt the ship move beneath their feet. "I must hurry, sir," exclaimed the boy, trying to slip out of the sudden firm grasp he felt on his shoulder. "You little fool, you're going to France with me," said M. Genolles.

"But I can't—I can't—my mother ..." stammered the frightened boy.

"Get back in your corner, and not a sound out of you, or you'll be beaten black and blue," was the only answer. The little boy, helpless, and seeing only unkind amusement in the faces of the other men, crouched in the corner, his face hidden on his knees, his fists pressed against his mouth, as he tried not to cry aloud.

One comforting thought sprang into his mind. His mother nearly always stopped to see him on Wednesdays, and this was Wednesday. If only . . . but it was a vague hope.

On Wednesdays, Wajelma's mother had a day's washing in the neighborhood of M. Genolles' house. As usual, on this Wednesday, she went early in order to have a few moments with her little boy. She hardly expected to find him waiting for her, as he was generally kept busy by his master. But the news given her by the servants was completely unexpected:

"Wajelma go to de ship wid massa. De ship gone. Wajelma ain't come back."

The poor mother dared not let her dismay stupefy her. She knew at once that Wajelma was probably kidnaped to be sold as a slave when the packet touched Baltimore, in the slave-State of Maryland. There was one person who might save her boy—Isaac Hopper, the Quaker, the last hope for many of the colored people, in cases just like this. There were many white friends of the Negroes, but Hopper was the most tireless of them all.

In a few moments the poor mother was pouring out her suspicions to him. On the instant, Hopper rushed out of his house to the pier only a few blocks away. But the ship was nearly out of sight.

He hurried back to his house and mounted his fastest horse. If he could get to Gloucester Point, three miles below the little Philadelphia of that day, before the ship should pass there, he had a good chance of getting aboard her. At Gloucester Point there was a ferry to take passengers across the Delaware River from Pennsylvania to New Jersey.

He had no spurs, no whip, but he dug his heels deep into the sides of the astonished horse, which lengthened into a faster and faster gallop. A bend in the road showed him the river. Good! He had gained! Luck was with him, for the packet had not yet reached the Point. He poured his story hastily into the ears of the woman who kept the ferry.

"Poor child!" she exclaimed. "Of course we'll help all we can. Here, John," she cried to one of the ferrymen. "Put Mr. Hopper aboard the packet as quickly as you can, and stay by him until he gets the boy who's being carried off."

The ferryman rowed toward the ship, Hopper standing in the prow of the boat, waving his wide Quaker hat, and gesticulating with his other arm. The captain took it for granted that here was another passenger for Baltimore, so he slackened speed, and, as the boat came alongside, ordered the sailors to help the late-comer aboard.

"Keep alongside the packet and watch for us," said Hopper to the ferryman as he climbed nimbly up the rope-ladder let down for him. The captain, bowing to his supposed new passenger, was given no greeting save the terse query: "Where can I find M. Genolles?"

"In the cabin, sir. May I ask——" But the sudden disappearance of Hopper down the companionway left the question in the air.

Hopper hastened to the cabin. There in the corner was the huddled form of the little boy, not even looking up in his despair. The group of men smoking and drinking around the table jokingly called to Hopper to join them. But instead he walked directly to M. Genolles, whom he knew by sight.

"My friend," he said, "what dost thou intend to do with the boy there?"

"Take him with me. He is my apprentice."

"True, but according to the laws of Pennsylvania, thou canst not take him with thee without having first obtained the consent of his mother, of himself, and of the magistrates. This thou hast not done."

"Fiddle; we are not in Pennsylvania now, and I have the boy. That ends it."

"No," said the Quaker. "It does not end it. The boy will go back with me. And as this packet is taking us nearer and nearer to Baltimore, we must leave it quickly."

"Captain! Captain!" he called loudly. The captain appeared in the companionway. "Put me and this boy into the ferryboat that is waiting alongside."

At first the captain refused. "Why should I trouble my passengers?" he asked.

"Thou shalt soon know," answered Friend Hopper, drawing from his pocket a book containing the laws of Pennsylvania. He opened it, and read aloud the law concerning kidnaping and its punishment. The captain was frightened. He saw that he himself would be involved if Wajelma stayed on the boat, so he finally said to Genolles, "You'll have to give him up."

"Go on deck," said Hopper to the boy, and Wajelma darted up the stairs like a flash. Genolles tried to catch him, but he ducked under the snatching hands. Hopper rushed after him, followed in turn by the entire party from the cabin, Genolles shouting violently, "You shall not take him!"

The ferryman in his boat below was watching anxiously for Isaac Hopper and the boy. When he heard the shouting he stood up in the boat, calling to them. Wajelma neared the rail. The man held up his arms, and caught the boy as he leaped. And only just in time, for Genolles' clutching fingers grazed the boy's shirt as he disappeared over the ship's side. Furious, the tailor turned on Hopper who was also about to slip over the rail, seized him, and began to beat him with his free fist. The others joined him, shouting "Pitch the meddler into the river!" The captain stood by, but offered no help to Hopper. Indeed, he seemed to be enjoying the affair.

But Hopper was strong and active. As a good Quaker, he would not exchange blows with the others, but, he thought, seizing a coat in his fist, "If I'm thrown into the water I'll take someone with me." A sharp blow on his arm automatically loosened his grip on the coat. But the next second he had grabbed another. This coat was pulled from him, and he laid hold on another, and another. It seemed as though the struggle might go on forever. But suddenly the right moment came. Hopper unexpectedly tore himself loose, evaded a violent blow, let go of the coat he had in his grip, and sprang over the rail. He fell in a heap in the waiting boat. Before he could disentangle himself, the alert ferryman had the boat yards from the packet, though not too far to miss the howls of rage from its defeated passengers.

Wajelma had been rigid with fear all during the struggle. Now he sobbed in relief, excitement and gratitude. "*How* did you find me?" he asked. "Oh, was it Wednesday and my mother's visit?"

"Yes, and she didn't waste a minute. Neither did I," chuckled the warm-hearted Friend. "Who'll be the happiest, you or she, when we get back to Philadelphia?"

THE ROAD TO CANADA

♥

For two hours, Allen had been keeping watch in the peach orchard near the road. Allen was only eleven years old, but he knew that his own home was a station on the Underground Railroad across Ohio. Sometimes he had seen a Negro man or woman come in, tired and hungry. His father and mother never told him how they came, or where they went. It was enough for him to know that they had been slaves, and were going to be free.

Today, he himself was part of the "Railroad," and he felt very proud as he looked down the road to the southward. That morning his father had said to him, "Allen, I am going to the far field to work. If any Negro should come along, thee can take him down to the corn-field, if thee likes, and hide him under the big walnut-tree. But do not tell me about it, or thy mother, or anybody else."

And so Allen played by the roadside, and watched for the runaway slave who might arrive. Surely enough, at last there came a poor fellow, with feet bleeding from the rough roads he had gone over, and clothes torn by underbrush he had broken through on his way to freedom. Hurrying along the road, he would pause each few yards, turn his head to listen, then hurry on again even faster than before.

Allen ran out into the road to meet him. The man started in terror at sight of a human, and looked from side to side, as if for a hiding-place. Allen spoke quickly:

"Is there somebody after thee?" he asked. "I'll hide thee, so that they cannot find thee."

"Yo' will? Can yo', for shuah? Is yo' Mista' Jay's boy?"

Allen nodded. The Negro grinned.

"Dey tol' me dat I'd get help heah. I'll go jus' where yo' says."

Allen quickly led the way among the trees of the orchard. Soon they were out of sight of the road, and the Negro looked back, sighing with relief. Beyond the orchard was the big corn-field, with rows of corn standing higher than the man's head.

"Nobody can find thee here," said Allen.

" 'Deed dey can't," answered the slave. "I feels *safe* now."

Farther and farther in among the rows of corn they went, until at last the great walnut-tree was reached, its branches spreading wide in every direction.

"Now thee stay right here," said Allen, "and wait for me. I will come for thee at the right time."

"I won't stir from heah," answered the man. "I'se been walkin' all day yest'day, and all night, an' I'se tired 'nuff to sleep till tomorrow come, ef I only wasn't so hungry."

"I will get thee something to eat," answered the boy, as he started back to the house.

He intended to go to the pantry, and help himself to some food for the fugitive. But when he reached the kitchen, he found his mother busy spreading slices of bread with butter, and laying cold meat between them. She looked up, as he entered, and smiled, but said nothing, and Allen sat down and watched as she packed a basket with sandwiches, cake, and fruit. Then she filled a jug with rich, creamy milk, and turned to him.

"Allen, if thee knows of anybody whom thee thinks is hungry, thee might take this basket to him."

Allen could hardly restrain his eagerness as he slipped off the chair and seized basket and jug. But he was rather amused, too, and he answered, with the slightest touch of a smile, "I will try to find somebody, but if I do not, I may eat the lunch myself."

"Very well," answered his mother, seriously, as he hurried out across the back-yard and over the fields to the great walnut-tree, where the colored man sprawled, resting his weary limbs, and watching hungrily for Allen's return.

The man ate as if he were starved. There was little left in the basket when at last he paused and poured out his thanks to the boy.

"I can sleep, now," he added. "I hasn't had my stomach full since I lef' ol' Virginny"; and indeed, as Allen turned away, he stretched himself out on the ground, and seemed to fall asleep on the instant.

Allen returned to the house and to his dinner. His father and mother chatted as usual, but the boy was unusually silent. He was thinking about the Negro lying under the walnut-tree, and wondering if he would get safely to Canada. He was soon to learn there were men who would do all they could to prevent this; for while the family were still at the table, two rough-looking men came riding up to the gate, and called loudly to Mr. Jay to come out. Obligingly, he obeyed their call, saying, as he left the room:

"They look like slave-catchers. I suppose they are searching for some unfortunate escaped Negro. Even if I had one sitting here at the dinner table, I should never give him up."

The Jay house stood rather near the road. Allen

slipped into the front room, and stood out of sight beside an open window. Here he could hear all that was said by the men on horseback, and by his quiet, self-contained father.

"Have you seen a nigger going by here today?" was the first question.

"No, I have not," came the reply.

"Don't let him fool you, Jim," interrupted the other rider. "The nigger didn't go past, because he came in. Look here, you Quaker, that nigger's in your house, and we're going to look for him there."

"There is no Negro in my house, but if it will give you pleasure to look for one, you are at liberty to do do so, provided you have the proper authority."

But this they did not have. They could only bluster and threaten, and finally rode away in disgust.

Afternoon passed without event. Supper-time came and it began to grow dark. Allen wondered more and more about what was to be done with the man. Surely he was not to be left under the tree all night. Then at last his father spoke:

"Allen, I have a basket of apples to send to thy grandfather. It is getting a little dark, but I think thee can drive over with old Ned, can thee not?"

"Yes, indeed," answered the boy quickly.

"I will harness the horse for thee, and put the apples in the wagon. It is only five miles, of course,

The Road to Canada » 33

but if thee would like to take anybody along, I shall be glad to have thee do so."

"Thank thee, father," said Allen quietly, as became his father's son. Catching up his cap, he ran through the kitchen door, and across the back-yard toward the corn-field and the walnut-tree. The Negro was still sleeping, but Allen caught him by the shoulder, and quickly roused him.

"Come," he said, "we're going on."

The man sprang to his feet, caught up the basket with its remains of lunch, and followed the boy to the barnyard. There stood old Ned, harnessed and tied to a tree, his head toward the road. Everything was ready for the start, but Mr. Jay was nowhere to be seen, and Allen knew that he was to drive away, without more words.

It was now quite dark, but Ned, a wise and experienced old horse, knew the road even better than did Allen, and trotted along at his own moderate pace. They met few people, and had no adventures of any kind before reaching the home of Allen's grandfather. Half an hour later, the Negro was astride a good horse, and trotting northward with another friendly Quaker beside him, on his way to the next station of the Underground Railroad. Months later, the Jays learned that he reached Canada safely.

"PRESIDENT" OF THE UNDERGROUND RAILROAD: LEVI COFFIN

"There's an underground railroad around here, and Levi Coffin is its president," said a slave-catcher, as he passed the plain home of Levi and Catharine Coffin in Newport, Indiana. The man had been searching for weeks for seventeen escaped slaves who had fled in a body from Kentucky. He and his companions had traced the fugitives across the Ohio River and for fifty or sixty miles through Indiana to Newport. The fugitives had not been actually seen to enter the Coffin home; therefore, the pursuers could get no search warrant to go through the house. But it was known that any slave who came to Newport might be sheltered by Levi Coffin. The slave-catchers watched the house for weeks, while at the same time searching all over the countryside.

But it was no use. The hot trail which had led to Levi Coffin's house ended right there, and the men finally went home in disgust, but leaving behind them the name that clung to this friend of Negroes for the rest of his life. It was so often repeated, in fact, that letters sometimes came to him addressed to "President of the Underground Railroad."

Levi Coffin's home was the converging point of several lines of the Railroad. Fugitives came to him from the East, from the West, or directly from the South, and were likewise sent on to several different stations, ten to twenty miles away. If word came that the slave-hunters were on one trail, the passengers were sent by another. More than once, a fleet rider was sent hastily to overtake a party of fugitives, warn them that danger was lurking ahead of them, and bring them back to Levi Coffin's hospitable home to wait until pursuit was given up.

Mr. and Mrs. Coffin never knew when passengers might arrive by the mysterious Road. But there was rarely a week that none did, and so they found it necessary to be always prepared to feed and care for fifteen or twenty people. There would be a gentle knock at the door, and Levi Coffin would spring from his bed to find a ragged, footsore man who had struggled northward alone for weeks, now brought to the Underground Railroad by a free member of his own race who lived nearby; or there might be a two-horse wagon loaded with fugitives. Quietly they would be led in, the door fastened, and the windows covered so that no light could be seen from without. Then the Coffins would build a fire, prepare food, and lay small mattresses before the fire for the Negroes to rest on the remainder of the night.

Frequently several wagon-loads from different lines of the Railroad came on the same night, by accident. The entire floor might be covered with weary men and women getting a little rest before they went on to the next station.

Once he was told that twenty-eight fugitives were hiding outside Newport. The next day Levi Coffin gathered together a number of carriages, loaded all the party into them, and sent a long, funeral-like procession on the road to Cumminsville.

Levi Coffin was born in North Carolina in 1798. Friends, even in that Southern State, had freed their slaves years before. But slavery was all about them, and the boy soon saw its horror and misery, and began early to do what he could to help its unfortunate victims. Gangs of slaves were often driven through North Carolina on their way to the cotton and rice plantations further south. Levi Coffin and his cousin, Vestal Coffin, would talk to these slaves as they rested at night. They could do nothing to help those who were legally slaves, but often they would find a kidnaped free Negro, whom they might help set free by legal means. One Negro who had been kidnaped from Philadelphia and sold in New Orleans was finally restored to his friends through information given by Vestal Coffin.

Many Quakers found it impossible to remain in North Carolina because of their anti-slavery sentiments. When they set their own slaves free, they sent many of them to settle in the free State of Indiana. Later the Quakers themselves in large numbers followed their old slaves. Before he was thirty years old, Levi Coffin and his young wife had settled at Newport, and had taken up their new method of helping the Negroes.

During the twenty years they lived in Indiana, they helped in freeing 3,300 slaves. An average of 106 fugitives a year slept under their roof. Readers of "Uncle Tom's Cabin" will remember the elderly Quaker, Simeon Halliday, and his kindness to fleeing slaves. Mrs. Stowe had Levi Coffin and his wife in mind when she wrote of Simeon and Rachel Halliday. Eliza, who crossed the Ohio River on blocks of floating ice, was also a real person who was sheltered in the Coffin home on her way to Canada.

In 1847, Levi Coffin started another form of service to the cause of freedom. He moved to the city of Cincinnati, Ohio, and opened a Free Produce Store; that is to say, a store in which nothing was sold that had been produced by slave labor. Such stores were already in existence in Baltimore and Philadelphia. Articles which came from the South, such as cotton, rice, and sugar, were of course more expensive if produced only by freemen, but many people were glad to pay the extra price.

Sugar could be obtained from Santo Domingo, the Negro island. Cotton was secured, by great effort, from small growers who owned no slaves. Rice could be done without, or obtained by the same effort. Levi Coffin made one trip, and possibly more, to Mississippi, to make arrangements for supplies of goods which had not been produced by slave labor.

Coffin's work was to continue even during and after the Civil War, for thousands of Negroes, set free, without means of livelihood, were in distress. Many had to leave the plantations, while others stayed on, but without employment. While the majority of Southerners took care of their former slaves as best they could, homes and plantations had been looted and destroyed during the war, and many former masters were as destitute as their Negroes.

Levi Coffin traveled over the country collecting funds and finally spent a year in England for the same purpose. Clothes, blankets, and $100,000 in money were given him by the friendly English to help the new freemen begin life again.

Until he was nearly eighty years old, he worked constantly for the colored people, and when he died they came in weeping crowds to say farewell. He had always lived according to what he once wrote in his journal:

"I read in the Bible that it was right to take in the stranger and administer to those in distress, and I thought it was always safe to do right. The Bible, in bidding us to feed the hungry and clothe the naked, said nothing about color, and I should try to follow out the teachings of the good book."

A STATION ON THE UNDERGROUND RAILROAD

♥

"Here dey come! here dey come! Look out fo' Suzy an' Flora!" A colored boy darted along the woodland path into the settlement of Cabin Creek, shouting a warning as he ran. But almost as his words were heard, the tramp of horses' hoofs sounded behind him, and a party of horsemen broke from the forest and trotted into the clearing. They were white men looking for two escaped slaves—whose names the boy-lookout was shouting.

Cabin Creek was a large settlement of free Negroes who had taken up land together in Indiana. Some of them had been born free in the Northern States. Some of them had bought themselves free from Southern masters, and many of these had relatives who were still slaves. All of them were glad to help any slaves who might reach them on their way to Canada.

The boy's shrill cry brought men and women hurrying from all parts of the settlement, gathering especially around one particular cabin. One of the horsemen pointed to this cabin. He was the marshal, the police officer of the neighborhood.

"I guess your girls will be there, Mr. Elwyn," he said. "That's where their grandparents live, and if you're sure they have gotten this far——"

"I don't know how they did it," answered the other. "They're only fifteen or sixteen years old, and it's two hundred and fifty miles from here to my plantation in Tennessee. I suppose they slept in the fields, and picked corn and berries by the way. But I knew they'd try to come here, and I've traced them. Yes, they're here, all right."

"It seems a pity to nab 'em, after they've walked so far, and as hungry as they must have gotten, to be free," said the marshal.

"Never you mind that. They're my property. I've spent money to find them, and to get this gang together to take them away from this nigger city. I mean to have them, and I want you to do your duty."

The marshal said no more, but jumped from his horse, and drew an important-looking paper from his pocket. This he opened and showed to the Negroes standing around the door of the cabin—half a dozen sturdy black men, and one old woman.

"This is my writ," he said. "The Judge gave it to me. It says that you must let us go into your house and take the two girls who belong to Mr. Elwyn."

"Yo' can't take 'em away," cried the old woman. "Dey is my own gran'chillen, an' I'll nebber let 'em go back to be slaves."

"You must do what the order says," answered the marshal, trying to push past her into the house. But the black men beside her stood like a wall, so he stopped. The slave-owner then ordered the Negroes to stand aside. "Get out of the way, you niggers," he shouted.

But they stood firmly. Then one of them said, "Sorry, suh, but we ain't yo' slaves. We'se free men, jes' as free as yo' is. If yo' wants to come in here, we mus' see de writ ourselves, an' know it's jus' accordin' to law."

The marshal handed the speaker the paper, which he read, slowly and carefully from beginning to end, while the slave-owner fumed and fretted. Meanwhile, a number of colored people slipped into the house— women, boys, one or two men—the guards opening a way for them while still blocking the whites.

The Negro with the writ now said: "Dis paper orders us to gib up de girls, Suzy an' Flora Elwyn, to dere master. Suzy an' Flora are my own nieces, an' I won't gib 'em up 'less'n I hab to. How do I know if he's dere master? How I know he's Mr. Elwyn?"

Again Elwyn broke out angrily, and tried to force his way through. But the marshal calmed him, and began a long argument with the Negro. Meanwhile, as they talked, every few moments colored people were coming and going from the house, until the slave-hunters paid little attention except to observe that the girls did not appear. Finally, the Negro seemed to give up.

"Will yo' promise dat de gals will hab a fair trial in court, if I lets yo' in?" he asked the marshal. The marshal promised, and the man turned to his mother. "It's de bes' we can do, mother," he said.

They moved from the door, and the marshal and the slave-owner rushed in. The other whites, waiting outside, expected to hear the girls scream in terror. Instead, they heard the swearing of angry men, as they searched in vain all over the cabin. The girls were not there! As the furious men came out, even their own companions burst out laughing. "The girls must have been let down through a hole in the ground to the Underground Railroad," shouted one.

None of the whites, however, could guess what a really bold and clever thing had been done. The girls were actually in the cabin when the party came up. But the Negroes had laid careful plans. The girls' uncle delayed the marshal at the door as long as he could. Inside, the girls were hastily dressing in boys' clothes, with slouch hats drawn down to shade their faces. While the talk went on, Negroes walked in and out, until the whites were accustomed to seeing them. Then the girls walked out with others, under the very nose of their former master.

Behind the trees and bushes a few yards away, two fast horses were standing beside a great log, each with a rider mounted. The girls in their boys' clothing had simply mixed with the crowd, and then slipped away, stepped upon the log, and jumped onto the horses' backs behind the men who were waiting for them. Starting off slowly, so as not to be heard, the horses were urged into a run as soon as it was safe, and carried the girls off at full speed. Their uncle, of course, knew when they came out, and as soon as they were safely away, let the slave-hunters go into the cabin.

For twenty-five miles the girls traveled, riding double with the horsemen, who were risking heavy fines or imprisonment for helping them. That evening they arrived at Newport, Indiana, and the home of Levi Coffin.

Levi Coffin and his wife, "Aunt Katy," took good care of the tired girls, gave them a hearty supper, and sent them to bed. They were sure there would be no danger that night. The next day, however, an-

other Negro rode from Cabin Creek saying that the slave-hunters had divided into small parties, in order to search all the Quaker towns nearby. One party was coming to Newport, he said.

Mr. Coffin was in his store when this word came. He hurried to his home to tell Aunt Katy to hide the girls. Then he went back to his store, so that he really would not know where they were if he were asked. Soon afterward, several strangers appeared in town, rambling around, asking about stray horses — which they could not describe very well — and bursting suddenly into homes of colored people. They walked up and down in front of the Coffin home, but did not quite dare to go in.

Even if they had done so, they were not likely to have found the girls. Aunt Katy had hidden them in a bed. There were no springs or hair mattresses on beds in the country, at that time. A large sack, the size of the bed, filled with clean rye straw, was placed over the bed-slats. Above this, another sack, or tick, full of feathers, made a soft and comfortable bed. Aunt Katy had the two girls lie between the ticks, carefully arranging the feather tick above them so they could breathe easily. Then she made up the bed, as usual, smoothed the counterpane, and put the pillows in place. The slave-hunters might suppose the girls were in Levi Coffin's home, but they were not sure, and so dared not go in, for fear that they themselves might be arrested. So that night the girls came out from between the mattresses, and slept in the bed in the ordinary way.

For several weeks longer, however, their former master was in the neighborhood, hunting for them. The Coffins never knew when their house was being watched, and the girls dared not so much as go to a window during all that time.

Finally, however, Mr. Elwyn gave up his search, and went back to Tennessee. Then Levi Coffin helped Suzy and Flora to the next station of the Underground Railroad, and they finally reached Canada in safety.

THE STORY OF FRANK QUAINTANCE

˅

LITTLE HENRY WILBUR swallowed his last mouthful of apple-sauce and gingerbread, and pushed back his plate. "Mother, may I go out and roll my hoop now?" he asked.

"Yes, for a little while," she answered. "But be sure to come in at once when I call thee, for it will soon be thy bed-time."

Henry seized his hoop from behind the door, and ran out with it into the pleasant summer evening. The plaything was only an old hoop from a barrel, but it was round and strong, and the boy had enjoyed many happy hours with it. Jumping down the porch-steps, he set the hoop down, and with his stick rolled it along the drive which led from the house to the road. It is hilly country in northern New York State, but the road at this point was level and straight, and a fine place for rolling a hoop.

Tonight, however, his game was cut short. He had made only one or two trips back and forth along his course, when he saw a horse, drawing a high-topped buggy, come trotting briskly along the road from the south. Henry stopped and looked.

"That's Jacob Pratt's horse, from South Easton," he said to himself. "I wonder if Jacob is bringing us an escaped slave." He stared at the two men on the seat. Yes, one of them was black. Dropping his hoop, the boy dashed for the house to carry the news.

The home of Job Wilbur and his son Humphrey, near Easton, New York, was a station of the Underground Railroad. It was nearly three hundred miles from the nearest slave-State, but it was on the road to Canada for numbers of slaves from the Carolinas and Virginia. Slave-catchers seldom pursued escaping slaves into northern New York; but when they did, they knew quite well that the Wilbur home frequently gave shelter to fugitives.

Henry had often seen colored men and women eating at his parents' table, or had known of their being hidden in haymow or orchard until they could be safely sent on to the next station. It was all a regular part of his six-year-old life. And so he now hurried to the house, calling to his father at the top of his voice. Humphrey Wilbur came out onto the porch.

"What is it, Henry?" he asked.

"Jacob Pratt is coming," panted the boy, "and he has somebody with him."

Humphrey turned back to the house, and spoke to his wife, who was in the kitchen with her mother-in-law.

"Ann," he said, "I think our guests will be hungry."

The two women had nearly finished clearing the supper table. Now they set things on again—applesauce, bread and butter and gingerbread, while Henry's grandmother hastily set the skillet on the fire, and began to cream a dish of cold boiled potatoes.

Presently the buggy came to the door, and two men stepped out. Jacob Pratt's passenger was a short, slim Negro, whom Jacob called Frank. The Wilburs made them welcome, and hurried them in for supper.

"We are truly hungry," said Jacob Pratt, "and yet I fear that Frank has little time to eat. I think a slave-catcher is on his trail. At the cross-roads, three miles back, we met a stranger on horseback who looked at us very sharply, and although Frank sat far back under the hood of the buggy, I fear he was seen."

"Sit down quickly," cried old Esther Wilbur, "and eat what you can."

"We must do more than that," said her husband.

The Story of Frank Quaintance » 51

"If that man was a slave-catcher, he may be here soon with others to help him. Jacob, thee had best start back at once over the same road. If Humphrey or I ride with thee, and we meet the man, they may think they were mistaken, and spare us a visit. If they do come here, we must do our best for Frank."

"I'll nebber be taken alive, suh," broke in Frank.

"Thee will not be taken," said Humphrey, reassuringly. Then, turning to the older Wilbur, he continued, "Thee is right, father. Thee and Jacob must go at once. If nothing happens, I will take Frank to Union Village as soon as he has had his supper."

The two men hurriedly drove away, Job carrying several generous slices of bread and cheese and gingerbread for Jacob's supper. Humphrey then turned to his small son who had been watching everything with large eyes.

"Henry, go and roll thy hoop up and down the road again. But keep a sharp watch, and if thee sees a stranger coming, just turn thy hoop into the driveway toward the house. Do not come in. I shall be watching, and will know what thee means."

Delighted to have the important post of watchman, Henry ran out to the road, and recommenced his game. But it was soon interrupted, for he saw two men on horseback riding toward him, on the road by which Jacob Pratt had come and gone.

One glance proved to him they were strangers. Shaking with excitement, he guided his hoop into the driveway and toward the house. Glancing ahead, he saw his father's face swiftly withdrawn from the window, and he knew that his warning had been received.

The riders galloped up and turned in at the gate where Henry stood, watching. In the house, meanwhile, there had been much commotion.

"It may not be they, Frank," said Henry's father, "but thee had better go up into the attic until we are sure. I will get the ladder, so thee can reach the trap-door."

He hurried through the kitchen to the woodshed where the ladder was kept. Frank followed at his heels. But as the two men started back with the ladder the Negro also snatched up the axe from where it lay in the shed.

"Frank, Frank, thee must not take that," cried the two Wilbur women together.

"I'll nebber be taken alive; nebber, nebber," answered the man, clutching the axe.

"Give me the axe, Frank, and thee hasten up the ladder," exclaimed Humphrey Wilbur. "We want no violence here."

"I won't use it less'n I hab to," answered the Negro. "But they can't take me alive."

He disappeared into the attic, letting the trap-door fall behind him. As Humphrey caught the ladder and hurried away with it, the two horsemen were drawing rein by the porch, and the next instant one of them knocked loudly. Henry's grandmother let them in, for they had a warrant to search the house. Every room was carefully examined.

"There's a trap-door," said one of them, finally. "Perhaps he's up there."

"No," said the other, "there wasn't time. They couldn't have known we were coming until we knocked."

"Just the same, I'm going to look," was the reply. A moment later he had placed the ladder, then he pushed open the trap-door, only to shrink backward in terror.

Above him stood Frank with the axe ready in his hands.

"Look out," cried Frank, "I doan' want to huht yo', but yo'll nebber take me alive."

There was nothing for the two slave-catchers to do but back down the ladder.

"We'll go now," they cried, "but we'll be back, and then look out for yourself."

They were hardly out of the house, however, before Humphrey Wilbur was helping the Negro to swing down from the attic opening. There would be a little time for them to prepare now, for the two slave-catchers had gone for help—they never loitered about singly. Wilbur's wife came hastening with one of her own neat gray dresses.

"Quick!" she said. "Get into this. Thee must get away with all speed." On went the dress, and the two women swiftly pinned white neckerchief and gray shawl into their proper places. The man's face was hidden in the tunnel-like depths of a Quaker bonnet, and it seemed hardly possible that this was the desperate Negro who, a few minutes before, had defied the slave-catchers with an axe.

Humphrey Wilbur was already in the barn, hurriedly harnessing the horse to a wagon loaded with potatoes. "The grocer in Union Village wants these potatoes tonight," he said. "It is Seventh-Day, and he keeps late hours. Thee shall go with me, Frank. Get in! Get in!"

The two climbed to the wagon-seat, and drove away in the gathering dusk, to all appearances a Quaker man and woman who were on the way to market in Union Village five miles to the north.

* * *

Henry pulled at his mother's hand. "Will he get to the next station all right?"

"I think so, dear."

"Shall we ever see him again?"

"Probably not; he will find work and a home in Canada."

But, much to the surprise of the Wilburs, they did see Frank again. Two or three years later, after the outbreak of the Civil War, when Negroes were comparatively safe in any part of the North, Frank came back to them, and asked for work on their farm. For a number of years, he was a most faithful and devoted helper, and Henry's close friend.

Henry heard from him many stories of slavery and of his escape to freedom.

"Thee ought to have another name, now, Frank," said Henry one day. "Now thee is free, thee should have two names."

"So I ought. Well, den, I'd like to take de name of Wilbur. Dat's de bes' name I know."

"But thee doesn't look a bit like us, Frank," said the boy. "People who have the same name ought to look something alike."

"Dat's so. Well, I'se made a lot ob good 'quaintances 'round heah. I'll just call myself 'Quaintance, —Frank 'Quaintance. How's dat?"

"That's very good," answered Henry. "Nobody else has a name like that."

And so Frank the slave became Frank Quaintance, the free man, and was known by that name from then on.

THE HEARTHSTONE

☙

THE THREE MURRAYS sat around their pleasant fire, each occupied in his own way. Mrs. Murray, by the light of a candle turned the heel of the woolen yarn stocking she was knitting. Her husband, with another candle on the little stand beside him, read aloud from the "Anti-Slavery Standard." Eleven-year-old Richard shook a long-handled skillet full of popcorn which he held over the coals, and listened happily to the sound of its popping.

"Here is the account of a slave-sale in Charleston," said Richard's father. "Mothers separated from their children, husbands from their wives. It is terrible work," he sighed, "but it cannot last."

His wife nodded. "The guilty ones will surely be punished. 'Vengeance is mine; I will repay, saith the Lord.' "

As she spoke there was the sound of feet on the

porch, and a knock at the door. John Murray laid down his paper, went to the door, and opened it.

"So you are at home, are you?" was the officious greeting which came from outside.

"Yes," answered Mr. Murray, gravely. "I am at home. Is there anything else that thee would like to know?"

"Not just now," was the visitor's reply. As he spoke, he brushed past Mr. Murray, and glanced into the living-room. Richard and his mother looked up in surprise, and the man stepped back to the door.

"Everybody is at home here," he said to his companions outside, and the party left the porch, with a word of thanks to Mr. Murray who in deep thought closed the door, dropped a heavy bar across it, and came back to his seat.

This happened in Ohio, about the year 1856. The Murrays and practically all their neighbors were strongly opposed to slavery. Whenever the marshals were on the track of an escaped slave, there were half a dozen Quaker homes here which were sure to be searched, and first of all the home of John and Hannah Murray.

John Murray looked thoughtful as he resumed his reading. After a few moments a second knock, much louder, sounded on the door. He sprang to his feet and looked at his wife.

"They have been to the stable and found the horses gone. Now they are sure there are slaves in the settlement, and they will search the house." He turned to the windows, and pulled down the shades, while Mrs. Murray dropped a cone-shaped tin extinguisher over the flame of each of the candles.

As the window-shades descended, a heavy blow shook the door, and an angry voice outside shouted: "Open the door! Open—in the name of the United States!"

"We are caught," said John Murray. "There is only one thing to do."

His wife darted from the room, while he spoke to the boy, who was excitedly watching the door.

"Richard, go upstairs, and wait until I call thee down. Then come quickly, and pop corn again, as though nothing had happened. Keep on popping, even though we do have visitors."

Richard hurried up the stairs. As he reached the top, he stopped in amazement, as he caught a glimpse of his mother coming quickly back to the living-room, leading a Negro by the hand.

"What is wanted?" Richard's father was calling to the men outside.

"You know very well what is wanted," came the reply. "We are after a fugitive slave. Open the door, or we shall break it in!"

"If you are peaceable, I will gladly let you in," answered John Murray, as he and his wife hurried the Negro into the room where they had just been sitting.

Richard stared in surprise from the top of the stairs. He knew that his father had not intended that he should see this, but he could not turn his eyes away, though he determined to let no word escape him to show where the fugitive might be. Where could they hide him in that room, anyway? There were no closets, nor large pieces of furniture which might conceal him.

As the boy stood puzzling, his father softly called him, and he hastened down the stairs, hearing all the while a rain of blows on the stout house-door. He hurried into the room, and glanced about. There was no sign of the Negro. His mother was lighting the candles again with a "spill," or lighter, from the vase of tapers on the mantel. The cat, which had been sleeping in a chair, was now curled up on the hearthstone close to where Richard himself had been standing. Where was the slave? But even as he wondered, he took up his skillet of popcorn and held it over the fire.

Outside, there was a shout, "Now, boys, all together!" There was a rush, and John Murray threw open the door, just as three men plunged against it and fell headlong into the hall, one of them breaking a chair as he fell.

The three rose quickly in much ill-temper. "We want that nigger slave, Mr. Murray, and we mean to have him," said the leader. "Here's a warrant for his arrest."

"We have no nigger slaves here, my friend; none but free people—as free as thee, and with much better manners. And as for thy warrant—where is thy warrant for breaking my furniture?"

"Search the house, boys," said the leader. "Don't pay any attention to the abolitionist."

"Give them a light, Hannah. Let them look; let them search thoroughly." This was spoken with a calm smile.

Hannah Murray handed a lighted candle to the men. "You should be proud of your business," she said. "You should be proud of chasing poor black people over the country, to carry them back to slavery."

The men hurried about their search, and the tramp of their feet sounded along the halls, and from room to room over the house. John and Hannah Murray took their seats again, and looked soberly into the fire, while Richard, upon the hearthstone, popped his corn carefully, although it was all he could do to keep from shouting with excitement.

Through the bed-rooms, the kitchen and the cellar the searchers went, but found no sign of the escaped slave; they muttered a few words of apology and left the house again. Hannah Murray took the candle from them, saying gently, as she closed the door:

"What would your mothers think if they knew you had descended to such work as this?"

The clatter of horses' hoofs sounded on the road. The men were gone. Richard could no longer contain himself.

"What did thee do with him, father?" he cried. "Where did thee hide him?"

"So thee watched?" asked his father.

"I didn't mean to; but mother came in with him before I was upstairs."

"Perhaps thee should know, now; but first let me see if any of our visitors remain on the porch or nearby." Mr. Murray stepped out, and looked carefully around. Finding nobody, he returned to the room.

"Now, Richard," he said with a smile. "I think thee has popped corn enough. Step off the hearthstone, and lift old Tabby back to her chair. Did thee wonder how she came to get down on the hearthstone?"

"A little, but I was thinking more about the man."

"I lifted her down myself," said his father, turning

back the rag carpet from the half of the hearthstone which it covered. "Now help me move the stone."

Together they turned the stone back. Here was exposed the entrance to a dark but roomy hole beneath the floor of the house. A small ladder was provided for descending. Several people might be comfortably hidden in the recess while search went on over their heads.

Richard peered in eagerly, while his father called: "Samuel."

"Yes, massa," came a voice from the darkness below. "Can I come up now?"

"Yes, I think it is safe for thee now."

John Murray held a candle over the hole. Richard was amazed that here in his own house was such a hideaway that his own exploring curiosity had not led him to discover before. How could it have been made without his knowledge? Perhaps at night while he was asleep. He looked at his father with beaming admiration.

Now *he* was big enough to be a part of the Railroad!

The Negro came quickly to the surface, and the hearthstone and carpet were replaced. Then John Murray said:

"Samuel, thee should know my boy Richard, who stood on the hearthstone above thee, with his cat sleeping beside him, and so turned the search away from this room."

The fugitive turned toward the boy, but Richard spoke quickly to stop the thanks which were coming. "I didn't know that I was doing it, but I'm glad if I did help."

DAVID GOES TO MARKET

❦

DAVID BUTTERWORTH drew a pencil from his pocket, picked up a pad of paper from the wagon-seat beside him, and scribbled two words on the top sheet. This he held up before his grandfather, who was holding loose reins over the back of the jogging horse. Old John Butterworth chuckled as he read the brief sentence.

"So thee is hungry, is thee?" He glanced up at the sun in the sky above them. "It lacks a good half-hour yet to noon. Can thee not wait until then before we get out the lunch basket?"

The boy shook his head vigorously, then held up one finger, which he moved meaningly.

"Just one sandwich, now; is that it?" asked the old man.

David nodded again, with much energy.

"Well, it was pretty early when we started; so I

don't wonder that thee is hungry. Yes; pull out the lunch-basket, and get thy one sandwich. But it won't be time for us to really eat for an hour yet."

David waited for no second bidding, but slipped down to the floor of the wagon, and began feeling under the seat for the well-filled lunch-basket. His grandfather kept the fat brown horse at its steady, jogging pace, and watched the boy smilingly, as he opened the basket, and took out the largest sandwich it contained.

David and his grandfather were on their way to market, with a load of newly-made brooms to sell. The old Quaker had been deaf for several years, and David often went with him on these trips, to help him in his bargaining. The boy had become skillful in writing one or two words to take the place of an entire sentence, and he and his grandfather had worked out a sign language of their own, which saved them much time and trouble in writing.

The Butterworths lived in the southern part of the State, not far from Cincinnati where they sold the produce of their farm — wheat, beans, wool, eggs, and home-made brooms. Sometimes the load bound for the market was a mixture of all these things; today the entire back of the covered wagon was filled with brooms. David glanced at these with pride. He had helped to raise the broom-corn from which they were made, and had done his share, also, in their actual making.

He closed the lunch-basket, climbed back upon the seat, and devoured his sandwich, while the wagon jogged on toward Cincinnati. The last mouthful, however, went down in a sudden gulp, for a man dashed around a bend in the road, and came running toward them at top speed. The man was almost coal-black; his woolly head was bare, his shirt and trousers in rags.

David's grandfather saw him at the same time. "An escaping slave," he exclaimed, "and with the slave hunters close on his track, too—he looks over his shoulder as if they might be upon him at any moment."

He shook the reins over the horse's back, and touched the animal with the old whip which he so rarely used that, even now, David stared in surprise. A moment later, the fugitive was beside them.

"Stop!" cried the old man. "Are they close behind thee?"

"Yassuh! yassuh! dey'll hab me in no time, shuah!"

The old man could not hear a word, but David nodded with all his might, as the Negro spoke.

"Quick, then," said old John Butterworth. "Get into the back of the wagon. Crawl under the brooms and hide thyself, and don't be frightened if we meet

thy pursuers." In an instant, the Negro had climbed into the rear of the wagon. He burrowed under the brooms like a mole.

Then David, struck by a sudden thought, slid off the seat and himself crawled under the brooms from the front.

John Butterworth, turning to lift and arrange the brooms over them, smiled in approval.

"Thee has done well, David," he said. "We are almost certain to meet the men who are after our friend; but as I shall not be able to hear a word they say, I shall not be able to answer them."

He looked on the seat for the paper, to toss it out of sight, but quick-thinking David had carried both paper and pencil with him under the brooms. A final glance at the pile of brooms, a touch to the horse, and the wagon went on once more, its only visible passenger a pleasant-looking old man taking a load of brooms to market.

They rounded the bend, and old John glanced cautiously about from under the shade of his broad straw hat. Just ahead, the road was intersected by another along which three men came galloping at top speed. The old man seemed to pay no attention to them. His horse jogtrotted past the cross-roads only a moment before the horsemen reached the same spot, all three shouting, "Stop! Stop!"

No sound reached the old man's ears; but the man and the boy under the brooms heard only too clearly the thunder of hoofs, as the horsemen overtook the wagon.

One of them seized the brown horse by the bridle and pulled him to a stop. Another, who had a small coil of light rope hanging from his arm, rode close to the wagon, saying violently, "Why didn't you stop when we called? Did you see a nigger back there on the road?"

"I am sorry, I cannot hear you, friends," answered John Butterworth. "Your business must indeed be urgent, since you stop a peaceful farmer by force."

The men looked at each other in disgust. "He's deaf," said the first.

"He's only shamming," said another. "I'll make him hear." Raising his voice to a yell, he shouted, "Did - you - meet - a - nigger - on the road?"

The old man smiled sadly. "It is no use to shout," he said. "I have not heard a word for five years."

"Come on, fellows," said the man with the rope. "It's no use. These Quakers will tell the truth about anything but a nigger. If he says he's deaf, he's deaf."

"Right you are," said the first. "We'll catch that fellow, though. He can't be far ahead." He let go the bridle, and with no further word, the three men spurred their horses into a gallop once more, and were gone on the back track. The two people hiding under the brooms heard the clatter of hoofs diminish and fade away in the distance. They dared not come out, however, until they heard the voice of John Butterworth assuring them that all was safe.

"Is he thanking us?" the old man inquired of David, for the Negro was gesticulating, and floods of words seemed to be pouring forth.

David nodded.

"What shall I do now, massa?" asked the man, finally.

David answered for his grandfather. "We'll set thee on thy way northward, of course." He turned to the old man, and scribbled on the pad: "Shall we take him to James Redstone?"

His grandfather nodded. "We are nearly there now," he said.

A few moments later they drove up to the door of a large white house which had sheltered many runaway slaves. Mr. Redstone himself came out to greet them.

"James," said John Butterworth, "we have brought thee a guest whom we met on the road, and were obliged to bring somewhat backward on his journey to the north." He told briefly of their experience with the Negro and his pursuers. "Now, friend," he added, turning to the Negro, "thee is safe, and will be helped from place to place on thy way to Canada. Farewell."

He turned his horse as he spoke once more to Redstone: "David and I are on our way to sell this load of brooms. We must make haste, or we shall be late."

David slipped back to his place beside his grandfather, and once more the two jogged along toward Cincinnati. A few moments passed, and then David hesitatingly wrote once more upon his paper.

"Yes," laughed the old man, "get out the lunch-basket. I am hungry also. It is past our dinner-hour now, and we have had a busy morning."

As he arranged the basket on the seat between them, David chuckled over his grandfather's phrase. It *had* been a busy morning for them. The afternoon would be a busy one for the Redstones. The boy's imagination followed the Negro northward, lying hidden by day in secret corners of Quaker homes, riding horseback by night, or being driven in a covered wagon from one station of the Underground Railroad to the next. Finally, Canada and freedom! David sighed with satisfaction, and it seemed to him that he had never tasted such a delicious sandwich.

A CASE OF
WHOOPING-COUGH

˅

A COVERED FARM-WAGON drawn by two horses pulled slowly along a sandy road in northern Delaware. It was a beautiful July day in 1853, and the strong farm-horses hardly needed to be guided as they went steadily along in their slow jog-trot.

The driver, however, seemed a bit apprehensive about something, and he frowned as he saw a man on horseback trotting briskly toward him. Then he seemed to gather himself to meet whatever might come.

"Good evening, Mr. Kent," said the rider, as the two met.

"Good evening, John," answered the other. Kent would have driven on without pausing, but the man John Frame had artfully stopped his horse so that Kent's wagon must stop also.

"Where are you going so late in the afternoon,"

asked Frame. "You are far from market and from home alike."

"I have a special errand," answered William Kent.

The other smiled knowingly, and added, "And you have a very special load of goods; or I am much mistaken."

"Well, yes," said the Quaker. "A miscellaneous assortment, and I must be driving on, for, as thee says, it is growing late."

But as he urged his horses on, the sound of a cough came from the back of the wagon. It was instantly stifled, as though a hand had been clapped over the coughing mouth. But the sound was unmistakable, and John Frame, leaning forward on his horse, laughed loudly.

"I thought I might find out something if I kept you talking long enough," he said. "Now I know for certain the sort of merchandise you are carrying." He laughed again, and spurred his horse, galloping off at top speed, giving the startled Quaker no chance to reply.

A voice now broke from inside the wagon—a woman's voice. "Oh, my Lawd," it cried despairingly. "Now us is lost, fo' shuah. Jim, you rascal, why cain't you keep yo' mouf shut?"

"I couldn't, mammy, I couldn't," answered a child.

"I held in, an' held in, an' when I t'ought I'd stopped it, de cough came out, befo' I know'd it." He coughed again, violently, as he spoke.

William Kent had set his horses going again on the northward road, but cast many uneasy glances behind him. Presently, the wagon neared a cross-road and he called back over his shoulder:

"I am sorry for all you folks tucked away there. I told you that we would reach our stopping-place in a half hour or so. But since we met John Frame, I feel that we must change our route, for I fear he has gone to give information about us. He would guess, of course, that we were on the way to Joshua Spencer's home, and the marshals will go there and search the place from top to bottom."

"We'll do anythin' you say, massa," exclaimed a man's voice, the speaker hidden from sight.

"Well, Frank," Kent replied, "if the children can stand it to sit there for another three hours or so, I will take you by another road, and to other good friends. It will be much safer."

"Yo' heah dat, chilluns," said the man, Frank, "yo' got to sit quiet heah, fo' a good while yit, or yo' may get cotched, an' took back."

"We'll be quiet"—"We'll be good"—"We don' wanta be slaves no mo'," rose a chorus of children's voices, accompanied by violent coughing.

A Case of Whooping-Cough   » 75

William Kent turned his horses into the crossroad, without further word, and drove on. For many minutes the only sounds were a burst of coughing from the sick child, or a suppressed whimper of "Oh, mammy, I'm so hungry."

"Keep up your courage," William Kent would then say to them. "We're getting nearer the place every moment."

And indeed, soon after nine o'clock, the wagon mounted a hill, and stopped before a pleasant farmhouse on the summit.

"Here we are," said Kent. He climbed down, and opened the wagon at the rear. Out came his passengers, cramped and stiff from their long ride—a Negro man, a woman, and three children. As they painfully descended, the house-door opened, and a handsome young Quaker couple appeared on the porch, smiling a welcome.

"James and Amelia Jackson," said the driver, "I wish you to know Frank and Sarah here, who are traveling northward with their children, Gus and Cassy and Jim."

Even as he spoke, and as the Jacksons greeted their unexpected guests, little Jim broke into a spasm of coughing which shook him from head to foot, and ended with an unmistakable "whoop."

"Whooping-cough," cried Amelia Jackson, turning pale. "What *shall* we do?" She looked up at her husband. "We cannot bring them into the house, on account of *our* children."

"The first thing to do," answered James, "is for Jim to keep as far away from Gus and Cassy as he can." He laid his hand on the boy's ragged shoulder, and drew him apart from the others. "And the second thing is for them all to have a good supper. As for their beds, the hay-mow is half-full of fresh, sweet hay, and there's no better bed in the world than new hay."

"Thy barn is perilously near the road," objected Kent, "and I warn thee there is danger."

"I think they are safe enough tonight," answered the farmer. "If the marshals are on the trail, they will spend themselves at the Spencer house. Our friends can sleep tonight, and tomorrow is another day."

James Jackson led the way to the barn, while his wife darted into the house, to prepare a hearty supper for the fugitives—plenty of homemade bread and butter, a great pitcher of milk, cold meat, cake, and blackberries. Presently Jackson returned for blankets and other things needed for the night. Back and forth he went, carrying bedding and food. At the last load, his wife followed him to the barn with a cup of "simmer," the old-time homemade cough syrup, of butter, brown sugar and water boiled down together.

A spoonful or two of this, taken whenever one felt inclined to cough, would soothe the irritated throat, and often stop a cough entirely. And it tasted good. Children of that day thought it was almost worth while having a cough, for the sake of the unlimited "simmer" that went with it.

So Amelia Jackson carried out a cup of "simmer" for poor little Jim, eating his supper in a corner of the hay-mow as far away as possible from his brother and sister. He coughed now and then, with a loud "whoop" which terrified his mother.

"Oh, Jim, Jim," she exclaimed. "Does it hu't you? Pore little boy! Oh, Jim, don't be sick. If you's sick we'll all be cotched, an' taken back."

"I won't be sick, mammy," answered Jim stoutly, and relieved her mind considerably by eating as hearty a supper as any of the others.

The meal over, the Jacksons helped their guests to make beds for themselves in the terraces of fragrant hay. The children, even Jim, dropped off instantly to sleep, and their parents seemed no less ready to rest as the Jacksons hung a lantern over a beam and said goodnight.

The next morning all were much rested and refreshed, though Jim continued to "whoop," and his mother, in terror of discovery, kept close by him, clapping her hand over his mouth at every outbreak.

Another cup of "simmer" came with the breakfast, and the Jacksons told their plans for the day.

"There are three or four families close by, all of whom work together to help our colored friends," said James Jackson.

"From this hilltop we can see the Hockessin valley for miles, and the road by which the marshal would come. I have visited all our neighbors this morning, and between us we shall keep a steady watch on that road during the entire day. If any strangers should be seen coming, we will be able to hustle you away to a safer place."

"But it might not be so comfortable as here," broke in Amelia. "So, unless there is immediate danger, you will stay here through the day. But you need not be afraid.

Thee can even let Jim cough when he has to," she added with a smile, turning to the anxious colored woman.

So throughout the long day, some member of the little Quaker community on the hill was constantly on watch. A messenger, sent to inquire at Joshua Spencer's home, brought back word that the house had been searched. Only William Kent's caution had saved Frank and his family from capture.

However, no searchers came to the Jackson home that day, and, as soon as it began to grow dark in the evening, the family were stowed away in the big wagon, with its large hood shielding them from passing view, and James Jackson drove them through the night toward the next station of the Underground Railroad.

"Even a mild case of whooping-cough can be very dangerous sometimes," Jackson smilingly remarked.

"CONDUCTOR" ON THE UNDERGROUND RAILROAD

♥

As young Thomas Garrett was returning on horseback to his home near Philadelphia late one afternoon in 1807, he saw his mother hurrying towards him, wringing her hands and crying. "Oh, Thomas, Thomas," she wailed, over and over again.

"What is it, mother?" he called.

"Nancy—— they've kidnaped Nancy!" she gasped. "Hurry over to the Judge's house and tell him, so he can send out officers to get her back."

"How long ago did it happen?"

"About an hour back. Oh, poor Nancy— And she's free, Thomas, as free as we are. How dared they?"

Thomas deliberated a few moments.

"They haven't such a great headstart. But it will take too long to find the Judge and get the officers out. I'll go myself, mother. Otherwise they may get so far away that we won't be able to pick up their trail. Luckily Darby here had an easy day," he said, stroking the horse as he looked carefully at the tracks in the roadway. "Here's another bit of luck! The wheels of the carriage have an odd pattern I can follow easily."

Jumping back on his horse, he galloped along the road leading south, following the trail with only an occasional stop to pick out the pattern after various other wheels had obliterated it.

"The trail keeps getting fresher," he said to himself. "I'm catching up to them."

He had gone some twelve miles when he found he could follow the trail without stopping to disentangle it, and then, a few moments later, as he rounded a curve he saw a carriage just ahead. The driver was whipping the two horses, and he heard a woman scream.

A second later she screamed again, but this time for joy as she recognized the horse and its rider who drew up alongside and seized the nearest horse of the team by the bridle.

The two kidnapers, slave-catchers by profession, made no trouble. They knew that even if they attacked and bound young Thomas, they stood small chance of getting out of the State, since their movements were known. They had counted on Mrs. Garrett being alone for several hours more. They knew they were liable to severe punishment if caught kidnaping a free Negro.

"You may as well get out and go back with him," they said roughly to Nancy.

Crying with joy, Nancy stepped out of the carriage, and Thomas swung her up behind him on his horse.

This experience made a deep impression on the boy of eighteen. It opened his eyes to the cruelty of slavery, and for the next sixty-four years of his life he did everything he could to help all Negroes, in slavery or free.

Garrett moved to Wilmington, Delaware, in 1822, after he had married. There he hid runaway slaves in his home, or would send them secretly to other workers on the Underground Railroad. If a new arrival did not seem to be closely pursued, Thomas Garrett would dress him in clothes like those worn by free Negroes in Wilmington. Garrett kept supplies of such clothing and of rakes, hoes, scythes, and the like, in secret places in his house. In the early morning, with rake or hoe over his shoulder, the escaping slave would walk briskly along the street. Nobody would pay the least attention to a Negro apparently going to his day's work. The Negro would hide the tool under a designated bridge to the north of Wilmington, and go on to the next station of the Underground Railroad. Later on, Garrett would stop

"Conductor": Thomas Garrett

by the bridge and pick up his tools. If pursuers came to Wilmington looking for the fugitive, they would find absolutely no trace of the ragged Negro whom they described.

Garrett was constantly under suspicion of having engineered escapes; but if he were directly accused, he would never deny it—he would only quietly refuse to give any information.

Once the Garrett home was surrounded by constables, watching for a Negro woman hidden there. Mrs. Garrett put one of her own dresses and a Quaker bonnet on the woman, and Thomas led her out of the house before the very eyes of the constables. She escaped, undetected.

Another time the Garretts were amazed to see two carriages, drawn by fine horses, stop before their door. They went out to greet their guests, and found eleven Negroes, who were fleeing from Chestertown, Maryland, fifty miles away. Harriet Shephard, the mother of five young children in the first carriage, was determined they should not grow up in slavery. She had persuaded five other Negroes to come with them. They had "borrowed" the carriages and horses, and simply drove off, starting at midnight. Late next day they reached Wilmington, asked the way to the Garrett home, and went directly there, without trying in any way to hide themselves.

Thomas Garrett did not like to hurry, but this time he hurried. Two carriages, four horses, eleven Negroes! The owners of all this property would soon be on the trail, and the trail was an easy one to follow. The horses and carriages he held, to return to their owners. The men, women and children he believed belonged to themselves, and they were taken instantly into Pennsylvania, where other Friends separated them into several parties, and sent them on to Canada.

It was about this time that an angry slave-owner pointed his gun at Thomas Garrett, declaring that he would shoot him if he did not tell what he had done with some escaping slaves. Garrett looked the man squarely in the face, and said only, "Shoot." Against such courage, the slave-owner was powerless.

Another time, two men came to Wilmington purposely to kill him and thus stop his assistance to runaway slaves. Garrett had been warned of their coming. Meeting them at his door, he said, "You men look hungry. Come in, and have some supper." Shamefaced and embarrassed, they accepted the invitation, and Thomas Garrett once again escaped harm. After the meal, one of the men thanked him, and went away. The other stayed, and worked for him for years.

Though Garrett thus escaped with his life, he

finally did lose his property. A reward of $40,000 had been offered by the Legislature of Maryland to any person who should catch him in the act of helping a slave, and then imprison him in any jail in the State of Maryland. That reward was never claimed, but in 1848, in Delaware, he was brought to court for helping a slave woman and her children northward. The judge knew him well, and offered to let him off if he would promise never to do such a thing again.

But Garrett replied calmly, "Thou hadst better proceed with thy business."

So the case was tried, and he was sentenced to pay a fine of eight thousand dollars. He had been having business troubles, so after paying this large sum he had nothing left. The local sheriff said to him:

"Well, Mr. Garrett, I hope you will never be caught at such work again."

However, to the sheriff's surprise, Garrett answered: "Friend, I haven't a dollar in the world; but if thee knows a fugitive who needs a breakfast, send him to me."

Fortunately, he had many friends, who helped him to begin business once more. In every Negro church in Wilmington the colored people prayed for their friend, that he might not remain in poverty.

Their prayers were answered. He was an old man,

but still with an excellent business head, and in spite of his continued activities for escaping slaves, he managed to accumulate another moderate-sized fortune during the next few years.

But the Negroes did more than pray for him. In the beginning of the Civil War there was rioting in Wilmington. Men who sympathized with the South made attacks on the homes of Negroes and of workers for the abolition of slavery. Unknown to the Garretts, the Wilmington Negroes kept a constant watch on their home, ready to call the police at a moment's notice, if there should be any trouble

In 1863, when all slaves were declared free by the Government, the Wilmington Negroes made a great procession of rejoicing for their people. They begged Thomas Garrett to take part, and the old man gladly consented. Great was his surprise, however, when the horses were removed from the open carriage in which he was riding, and he found himself drawn by a dozen men at the head of the procession. Before him there marched another man carrying a banner on which was written, "Our Moses."

This was the climax of Garrett's great work for Negroes. His colored friends still came to him often for help and advice, but there were no more terrified men and women or families knocking at his door, begging him to save them from slavery. "The Government has taken over my business," he said, after the war broke out. "Now I can retire." Then he added, wistfully, "I have helped only twenty-seven hundred slaves to freedom. I had hoped to save three thousand."

BROWN SISTER

❧

ONE BRIGHT SUMMER MORNING in southern Ohio, sunlight creeping across her face woke thirteen-year-old Lucinda Wilson at about five-thirty o'clock. She sat bolt upright, and then made a leap out of bed as she thought, "The strawberries on the hill must be ready to pick." Lucinda had been watching with eager eyes a hill overgrown with wild strawberries. Now she joyously planned to surprise the family at breakfast with a basketful of the luscious, ripe berries.

She dressed rapidly but quietly so as not to disturb her sleeping sister. Lucinda had had the big bed to herself that night, as seventeen-year-old Mary was spending a few days with a chum on a nearby farm, and Ruth, the fifteen-year-old, slept on a narrow cot under the eaves at one end of the big upstairs room.

The Wilson house stood some distance back from the main road, with a long, straight drive from the gate to the front door. The drive seemed much too long to the girls on foot walking it, so Lucinda took a short-cut to the strawberry hill which lay along the highway, a path leading out of the barnyard, almost invisible in the tangle of growth. Lucinda hurried along the path to the road, and started up the hill. There were the berries, just as red and delicious as she had hoped. She began to pick rapidly, but the bottom of her basket was not even covered when a voice called to her from the highway below.

Startled, she looked down and saw two men on horseback. They were strangers to her, and her first glance put her on guard, for her home was a station on the Underground Railroad. These men, she felt certain, were slave-catchers.

The next instant Lucinda knew she was right. The man who had called to her, dark and scowling, now spoke again, "Have you seen two black girls go past here?" he asked. "Two girls about seventeen or eighteen years old? They're only a few minutes ahead of us, we're sure."

Lucinda shook her head. She answered them honestly that she had just come to the spot, and had seen nobody but themselves.

The men touched their horses and moved on. But Lucinda had no more thought of berries. The two girls would come to her home, she was sure, and the men would catch them at the very door, unless they were warned. She looked cautiously after the riders, to make certain neither was glancing behind; then she darted across the road, and ran back along the path.

In a few moments, she was in the farmyard, and hurrying to the house. As she tore open the backdoor, she heard her mother's voice at the front. The Negro girls had come, and the men would be there the next instant. Breathless, she burst upon them. The door was still open, the girls and her mother standing in the hall.

"Shut the door! shut the door, quick!" she gasped. "They're coming after you!"

Even as she spoke she saw a horse turn into the driveway. Mrs. Wilson slammed the door, locked it, and looked wildly around for a hiding-place for the two trembling colored girls.

"Oh, dey'll drag us back again. We'll nebber be free, nebber!" cried one of them.

"Hush!" said Mrs. Wilson. "Go upstairs. *Quick!*"

They rushed up the stairs, and into the room where Ruth was now up and half-dressed. She looked up, startled, as the four burst in.

"Lucinda," her mother directed, "put on thy nightcap and night-gown again, and get into bed."

She seized Mary's night-clothes from under the pillow, and thrust them upon one of the colored girls. "Put these on, and get into bed with my daughter. Lie next the wall, and turn thy head away from the door. Pull the cap well down over thy face."

As the girl hastened to obey, Mrs. Wilson lifted the top of a large square wicker clothes-hamper which stood at the side of the room. Fortunately, it was nearly empty.

"Get in there," she said to the other girl, who stepped in, and crouched down for the lid to be replaced.

A loud knock sounded at the front door. "Sit on the basket, Ruth, and catch thy dressing-gown around thee. The slave-catchers will be up here in a moment."

Mrs. Wilson glanced around the room. There was nothing in sight to show that the colored girls had been there, and she hastened down the stairs to open the door.

"Good morning, ma'am," said one of the men. "We're after those two nigger girls that you have here."

"Indeed," she answered, "and how does thee know that we have two Negro girls here?"

"Because we were right on their heels, and we know they wouldn't have gone past here. So you'll have to let us search the house."

"You are welcome to do so, if you wish. But I can assure you that it will be wasted labor. You will find no Negroes here."

"We'll see about that," answered the man, as the two began a thorough search of each room in the house. Mrs. Wilson let them open the doors, and look as they would, until they came to the girls' room. Then she stepped forward.

"My three daughters sleep there," she said, "and it is yet early morning. Gentlemen, I beg you not to enter their room."

"Just as likely to be here as anywhere," said one of the men, and he opened the door and went in. There were the three girls, two in bed, with the bedclothes pulled up to their ears; the other sitting upon the wicker hamper, holding her wrapper about her, as though taken by surprise. In the hamper under her, however, the terrified colored girl was trembling so that it seemed to Ruth the men must see the hamper shaking. She sat as heavily as she could, and covered the hamper with her wrapper as far as possible.

Somewhat embarrassed, the men looked hastily about the room, opened the closet-door, and finding nothing, went out again, with a half-hearted apology.

"Well," said one of them, as they came from the last room, "it begins to look as though those girls went past here, after all. We'd better put on speed, and perhaps we can overtake them yet."

"I told you that you would find no colored girls here," said Mrs. Wilson, quietly. She then hospitably offered them breakfast, but they refused in their haste. They galloped off and the girls were free to come from their hiding-places.

"De Lord bress you, missy," said the girl who had been Lucinda's bedfellow during those tense moments. "You saved us, shuah."

"I'm glad I decided to pick strawberries for breakfast," said Lucinda. "And it's still early enough for me to go back and fill my basket. We'll have some for breakfast, after all."

The two colored girls stayed quietly in the house all day. Late that night a covered wagon took them to another Quaker home on another road. From there they were sent on next day with little danger, for word had come back that the two slave-catchers had lost all trace of them and declared that they had burrowed underground.

THE RUNAWAY SLAVE

❧

LUCINDA WILSON hurried along the country road toward her home, wondering if she would be in time to ride the first load of hay. There was nothing more delightful, Lucinda thought, than riding from the hayfield into the barn, perched high upon a load of new, sweet-smelling hay. She had wanted to go into the field with her father and his helpers immediately after their mid-day dinner, but her mother needed her for an errand first.

One of their neighbors was ill, and Lucinda's mother and several other friendly housewives were helping the family by sending in bread and butter and hot dishes of meat and potatoes.

Lucinda did her errand faithfully. She slipped quietly into the Myrick kitchen, put three loaves of bread in the pantry, and the closely-covered bowl of butter in the cool cellar. Then she tiptoed upstairs, to ask how Mrs. Myrick was feeling.

Stories of the Underground Railroad » 95

"Mother will be here tonight to stay with her," she told the neighbor who was acting as nurse at the moment.

In those days trained nurses were little known. People took care of one another, and if a member of a family was sick, friends and neighbors came in by turns to help with the nursing.

Her friendly errand done, Lucinda was now free for her hay-ride. She walked swiftly down the maple shaded road, glancing behind her occasionally, down the road coming up from the south. This was the road on which fleeing slaves usually arrived, and in her fancy she was always expecting to see such travelers, so she was not surprised, as she turned into the short-cut path to her home, to see a man running toward her from around a bend in the road. He was light brown in color and might be mistaken at a distance for a white man, but his terror identified him as an escaping slave.

Lucinda waited for him to come near, and then called to him, "Is there somebody after thee?"

He stopped suddenly. "Yes, Missy; dey's close behin' me. Whar can I hide?"

"Come with me, quick. Father will know what to do."

He hurried after her into the short-cut path, and a moment later its windings hid them both from sight of the road. The two men who came galloping up just as they disappeared did not realize that the slave had taken to the faintly marked path.

"That fellow runs well," said one of them. "He's around that next bend already."

"He's making for Wilson's, of course," answered the other. "I've lost a dozen niggers there, or more. They seem to disappear from the earth. But we ought to catch this fellow before he gets to the door, and they won't have time to hide him, for once."

The two slave-catchers spurred their horses, and galloped on.

Meanwhile, the poor fellow whom they meant to catch was racing along the path, closely following Lucinda's flying feet. He was covered with dust, his clothes were the roughest of slave-clothes, and he was so tired that he staggered as he ran. Both of them glanced over their shoulders at first, but nobody pursued, so they relaxed their pace a bit.

They hurried through the barnyard, and out into the great meadow behind. Lucinda had feared her father might be at the far end of the field, but to her joy, the wagon stood near the barn, her father and another man pitching hay up to a third man, who received and tramped it down on the load.

"Father!" she cried out. "Father!" Her father started; then dropped his pitchfork and hurried to

them. "Hide him, quick, father," she urged. "They were close behind him, and we ran through the path. They didn't see us, but they're near."

"Through the path," said her father, thoughtfully. "If they did not see you, they have gone to the house. They will search the house, first, and then come out to the barn, and look for me. We have at least five minutes yet." He looked carefully at the Negro, then stepped up to him, lifted one of the man's hands, and held his own sunburned hand beside it. There was hardly any difference in shade.

John Wilson smiled. "We can do it," he said. "Can thee pitch hay?"

The man nodded.

"Come, then," said Mr. Wilson. He hastened into the barn, the fugitive at his heels. A moment later, they were out again. But in that moment, the Negro's appearance had been completely changed. A full suit of Mr. Wilson's overalls covered his torn and dirty clothes. A broad-brimmed straw hat, such as the hay-makers were wearing, hid his woolly hair and the back of his neck. In his hand he held a pitchfork.

The two men strode out to the hay-wagon. Lucinda hesitated a moment about following them, but her father called to her to come. "I have another hand today," he said. "The wagon will be loaded in no time, and thee shall have thy ride."

The Runaway Slave

The next moment four men were working where three had worked before. Forkful after forkful of hay was tossed to the load. The newcomer was as skillful as any of the Quakers. Then came a loud hail from the barn-door. A man was standing there, calling to Mr. Wilson. Lucinda's father dropped his pitchfork and went toward him, Lucinda following in order to hear the conversation.

"Say, Mr. Wilson," said the slave-catcher, "you've got a runaway nigger here, and we're after him. Where is he?"

"Thee knows very well that even if I had an escaped Negro here, I would never tell thee where to find him."

"The fellow was just ahead of us. He must have come into your place. My partner and I have gone through the house, and now he's searching the barn. Who are these men you have out here?"

"Thee can see for thyself," said Mr. Wilson, calmly.

The man came out of the barn, and walked a few steps toward the great wagon with the three overalled workers busy around it. Lucinda, turning to watch them, noticed how dexterously the Negro kept his back to the slave-catcher, or when he turned to toss up a forkful of hay, kept the hay before his face for the instant it might have been seen.

The man stared in every direction over the field. Nobody was in sight except the busy workers by the hay-wagon, and the little girl waiting to ride on the load.

The three sunburned men were dressed alike in overalls and broad-brimmed hats. There was no ragged and woolly-headed Negro to be seen, and so he turned away with an exclamation of disappointment.

"Bill," he called to his partner in the barn, "I don't see that fellow anywhere out here. Either he went past this place after all, or else he's gone underground like those others."

"He's nowhere in the barn, sure," answered the other, coming to the door. "I've been all along the haymow and looked in every stall and feed bin."

"What about the mangers?" asked his partner.

"I pulled a horse's or a cow's nose out of every one of them. Nothing doing."

"You don't suppose he might be wearing a little girl's clothes?" he said with a sarcastic grin, looking at Lucinda.

"Come on," was the reply. "We don't have time to be funny."

Angrily the two men rode away, leaving the escaped slave in comparative safety.

The mulatto wished to stay and work to show his

gratitude, but Mr. Wilson reminded him that this was only a breathing spell and not freedom and he must continue on for his own safety—for the Wilson home was a busy station on the Railroad.

That night, washed and fed, he slept in a comfortable bed in the Wilson home, and the next day, dressed in clean clothes, was sent on his way toward Canada and freedom.

THE FACE AT THE WINDOW

❦

TEN-YEAR-OLD JAMES MATLACK came running into the sitting-room where his parents were relaxing by the evening fire.

"Father," he cried in excitement, "the horses are gone from the stable! Somebody has stolen them!"

His father, James Matlack, Sr., looked up and smiled. "Do not trouble thyself about it," he answered. "I have found the horses gone quite often, when I went to the barn after dark. But I always go to bed, and sleep very soundly, and in the morning they are back again safe and sound. They may be a little muddy, and need the currycomb, but they are always quite safe."

"But, father, how——" The boy paused, puzzled.

"I think that Jamie is old enough to be told," his mother interposed.

Her husband nodded. "Thee knows, my boy, that

Negroes often pass through the settlement, on their way north to Canada. They are escaping from slavery, and they endure every hardship, that they may win their freedom. There is a law now that if they are caught anywhere in the United States, they must be returned to their owners. People who help them are liable under the new law to be punished."

The boy, listening eagerly, burst out: "The Friends would never send a man back to be sold just like a horse or a cow!"

"No, we will not," answered his father. "Friends wish to obey the law of God, as above the law of man, and we will help these colored people who come to us, in every way we can. Why should fear of suffering keep us from doing what we think is right?

"Negroes who come to me or to Neighbor Coates are helped on their way. They are often driven twelve or fifteen miles northward to another Friends' settlement, where they will be helped further."

"But how, father?" cried the eager boy. "Thee never takes them, I am sure. Thee is always here every night, and in the morning, too."

"That is true," was the smiling answer. "I am always here nights. So it is quite impossible that I should take slaves northward. I am at home, even if my horses are not."

"But where are the horses?"

His father continued: "And if anybody should think of charging Neighbor Coates with taking runaway slaves northward, they might perhaps find Joseph out for the evening; but they would find his horses in their stable. It hardly *looks* as though either of us could have anything to do with such things . . ."

Jamie's eyes were fastened questioningly on his father for a moment; then he burst out, gleefully: "Oh, I see now—Friend Coates takes thy——"

"Hush!" interrupted Mr. Matlack. "Do not even speak it. Neighbor Coates and I are partners in a plan for sending marketing northward, that is all, and we do not even talk about that. Thee had better shell some corn for thy hens, now."

He turned again to his paper, and Jamie obediently brought in a basket of corn, and, sitting down on the hearth, began to rattle the kernels into a tin basin. His eyes wandered about as he worked, now upon the fire, now upon its reflection in the unshaded window.

Suddenly he started. He had caught a glimpse of something moving outside the window. The next instant a coal-black face was pressed against the pane. The appearance was so sudden that Jamie dropped his corn-cob into the basin, and uttered a sharp exclamation. His father and mother looked up in surprise, as a black hand opened the window a bit, and a voice said: "Please, missus an' massa, don' be scared. It's only a poor cullud man."

The elder Matlack sprang to his feet, and went to the door, coming back a moment later with the blackest Negro that Jamie had ever seen. He gave the man a seat by the fire, while his wife hurried out to the kitchen to get some supper for the traveler. Then Mr. Matlack questioned him.

"Where is thee going?"

"Dunno, massa. I'se jes' follerin' de Norf Star till I'se free."

"Is there anybody following thee?"

"I don' think so, massa. Twenty, thirty mile back, I cut across from one road to anudder, an' I think I fooled 'em dat way, if anybody was a-follerin' me."

"Yet there is always danger, and it is well to go on as rapidly as possible. Thee can eat here and sleep for a while, and then we can send thee on further this very night."

"God bress you, massa," exclaimed the slave, in gratitude.

Mr. Matlack turned to Jamie. "Jamie, I wish thee would run over to Neighbor Coates, and tell him that I have some more marketing for him tonight, and will bring it over about one o'clock."

The boy jumped up, seized his cap, and hastened on his errand. His heart was full of exultation. He was old enough now, and so trustworthy, that he was taking part in this great enterprise. He was carrying a message that would help a man to freedom.

Neighbor Coates' home was not far away, and the message was soon delivered. Jamie returned home, to find the Negro already fast asleep, and his father was locking the house for the night, to insure the safety of the refugee.

"Can I take him over to Neighbor Coates, father, when it is time?" asked Jamie, eager to do all he could in this thrilling business.

But his father shook his head. "No, son, thee has done thy part. All thee can do now is to go to bed, and to sleep."

"But, father, won't thee anyhow please wake me up, and let me see thee take him away?"

Mr. Matlack smiled, but seeing the boy's earnestness, promised to do so.

And so at one o'clock in the morning a very sleepy Jamie, yet wide-eyed with interest, came part way down the broad stairs to watch his father start out with the Negro, who was wearing an old coat of Mr. Matlack's to add warmth to the thin garments he had fled in.

His father pointed to the boy. "My son wants to wish thee good fortune," he said to the Negro.

The Negro, grinning with pleasure, pulled off his

worn hat, and called back, "Thanks, little massa, thanks. Now I knows I shall reach de Promised Land."

"Goodbye," said Jamie. "Goodbye; I hope thee will reach Canada soon."

The door closed, and Jamie stumbled back to bed, happy, because another man would soon be free.

"ENGINEER" WHO NEVER LOST A PASSENGER: HARRIET TUBMAN

❦

HARRIET TUBMAN was considered the bravest of all the Underground Railroad workers. There were many, both whites and blacks, who ran risk of fine and imprisonment while helping escaping slaves or taking them into their homes. But Harriet Tubman faced death or worse than slavery, for she herself was an escaped slave, who dared go back to the South again and again to lead her people out of bondage.

She was born in Maryland about 1821, and grew to be a strong, sturdy woman who could plow, drive oxen, and chop a half-cord of wood a day. One day she and her two brothers learned that they had been sold, and would be taken further south the next morning. They decided to run away that very night, and try to reach the free North.

Of course they dared tell nobody what they intended to do, but Harriet wanted to say goodbye to her friends in some way. So as she passed their cabin doors, she sang an old spiritual:

> "When that old chariot comes,
>   I'm going to leave you.
> I'm bound for the promised land,
>   Friends, I'm going to leave you.
>
> I'm sorry, friends, to leave you,
>   Farewell! Oh, farewell!
> But I'll meet you in the morning,
>   Farewell! Oh, farewell!"

When the overseer was nowhere near, she would revise the last lines and sing them significantly:

> "I'm bound for the promised land,
>   Farewell! Oh, farewell!"

The next morning Harriet was gone, and her friends knew that she had been saying a real farewell. She and her brothers started out together as planned, but the brothers became afraid of the consequences of recapture, so they turned back. Alone, Harriet followed the North Star all night long. At dawn she lay down in the tall grass of a swamp, and at night went on again. So she traveled, walking at night, hiding by day, begging food from Negroes, or going hungry. At last she reached Philadelphia, where she felt safe.

She found work, and saved every penny she could. As long as her father and mother were still slaves, she felt herself only half free. So, as soon as she had a few dollars in her pocket she went back to Maryland, hiding by day in swamp or forest, as before, and walking by night. Straight to the old plantation she went, and was hidden in the cabin of one of her old friends. How they listened as she told about the free country—where a black person could sell his labor, just as if he were white!

Her parents were afraid to try to escape, but a number of others followed her. They forded rivers, climbed mountains, went through swamps, thickets, forests, always hiding by day and walking by night, often with sore and bleeding feet. But they escaped to freedom.

Harriet knew the way now, and knew some of the stations of the Underground Railroad. She started in again to earn money and prepare for another trip. Again she reached her old home, and again she tried to bring her father and mother away. But still they refused, and she was obliged to go without them, although another large party of slaves did go north with her.

The third time she came back to the plantation,

she was so sure of taking them safely through all the dangers, that the old people dared at last to come. But, according to the story, her father insisted that he must take his best hen-coop, while her mother could not leave without her feather-bed.

"How can we travel with such big things as those?" exclaimed Harriet. But the simple old people could not be parted from them, and so Harriet found a horse and a two-wheeled cart; loaded in father, mother, feather-bed and chicken-coop, and started north.

In spite of a white patrol which guarded the roads night and day, to catch runaway slaves, the party managed to get through without event. They reached Delaware, and went directly to the home of a Quaker, who gave them food, shelter, shoes all around, and money to get to Canada. However, no sooner were the old people safe than Harriet was back on the trail to lead more slaves northward.

For fifteen years she kept this up, and made nineteen trips into Maryland, leading over three hundred slaves away. With every trip the danger became greater, as her activities became more generally known to the planters. The patrol was more vigilant than ever, and the price on her head was steadily increasing. Finally notices were posted throughout the State, offering $40,000 for her, dead or alive. Any slave who would betray her might have claimed freedom for himself and his family, besides more money than he could imagine, but no slave ever dropped a hint that might endanger their deliverer.

Again and again her parties escaped capture by hairbreadths. Once they stood up to their necks in water for hours. Once they dug holes for themselves in a sweet potato field. Often there were women with babies in the party. A crying baby might have betrayed the entire group. For safety, Harriet always carried a bottle of paregoric, and drugged the babies until they slept quietly without crying.

On one trip she came to the home of a Negro who had helped her several times before. She left her party behind, and gave the peculiar rap which was her signal. But there was no answer until she had knocked several times. Then a white man gruffly asked what she wanted, then told her that her friend had been obliged to leave town for assisting runaways.

Morning was near and there was great danger. Harriet knew no one else in the town. She hurried her party away, and they hid in a swamp nearby. All day they lay there, cold and hungry and wet, Harriet praying constantly for help.

It began to get dark, and then a man in Quaker costume came walking slowly along the pathway on

"I'M BOUND FOR THE PROMISED LAND, FAREWELL! OH, FAREWELL!"

the edge of the swamp. He seemed to be talking to himself, but Harriet was looking for deliverance, and she listened keenly to his words.

"My wagon stands in the barnyard of the next farm across the way," said the Quaker to himself. "The horse is in the stable; the harness hangs on a nail beside him." He went along the path and was gone.

As soon as it was fully dark, Harriet slipped away and went to the barnyard. There was no person near, but there were the horse, the harness, and the wagon, and the wagon was loaded with food. Soon the entire party was on its way rejoicing, and no longer hungry. They did not drive far, however. Harriet knew a Quaker in the next town, and asked him to return the horse and wagon to its owner. How he had learned the party was in the swamp, she never found out. Perhaps he did not know certainly; he might have made ready the horse and wagon, and talked to himself about them on the mere chance that there were fugitives hiding by the pathway. Or possibly the gruff man in her friend's house was more sympathetic than he seemed!

Finally, not long before the Civil War, Harriet bought a little house near Auburn, New York, and settled there with her parents. One after another, old, homeless Negroes came to her, and she took them in until she was trying to support twenty old people.

There was a mortgage on the place, and she did not have money to meet it. "Let me write the story of your adventures," said a friend. So they set to work. It took a long while, for each day Harriet would think of some exciting incident that she had forgotten. But the book was finished at last, and enough copies were sold to pay the mortgage, and to make sure that Harriet's house should be an Old Folks' Home, even after she could no longer work for it.

Harriet Tubman died at the age of ninety-two. The city of Auburn held a great memorial meeting in her honor, and placed a bronze tablet in tribute to her in the county courthouse. On this tablet is written one of her sayings: "On my underground railroad I never ran my train off the track, and I never lost a passenger."

CPSIA information can be obtained at www.ICGtesting.com
Printed in the USA
241757LV00001B/259/A